Everything for Love

Victor, L. Sabadus

WestBow
PRESS®
A DIVISION OF THOMAS NELSON
& ZONDERVAN

WestBow Press books may be ordered through booksellers or by contacting:

WestBow Press
A Division of Thomas Nelson & Zondervan
1663 Liberty Drive
Bloomington, IN 47403
www.westbowpress.com
1 (866) 928-1240

ISBN: 978-1-5127-6487-1 (sc)
ISBN: 978-1-5127-6486-4 (e)

Library of Congress Control Number: 2016919452

Print information available on the last page.

WestBow Press rev. date: 12/15/2016

1   **EXT.(EXTERIOR) COUNTRY BRIDGE - NIGHT**

FADE IN:

A "WATER OVER BRIDGE" road sign is pounded by rain. We crane up from the sign to reveal a covered Amish buggy slowly making its way over a washed-out bridge; wheels buried halfway in water. A bright light-post lights up the bridge.

A red Porsche approaches the buggy on the opposite direction and passes the buggy. Moments later the car hits the water over the bridge and spirals out of control, hitting a tree. It ricochets off the tree next to the river's edge.

2   **INT.(INTERIOR) JAKE'S PORSCHE - NIGHT**

The water rises quickly as JAKE Daniels, a white man in his early 20's, is passed out cold.

                                        FADE TO BLACK:

VOCAL FAITH SONG BEGINS...

FLASH ON SCREEN: "One Day Earlier"

FADE IN:

3   **INT. RITZY HIGH-RISE/JAKE'S APARTMENT - NIGHT**

OPENING CREDITS FLASH ON SCREEN...

We see a super close-up montage of a painting being created. Brush stroke after brush stroke of different kinds of colors. Brush dipping into the paint, and so on... We see other paintings hanging on the wall, all modern art type.

At the end of the montage, Jake stares at his newly painted creation. Only the back of the frame is visible.

VOCAL FAITH SONG ENDS.

Phone vibrates on the table. Jake answers on speakerphone.

                        JAKE
              What's up, Gina?

                        GINA(V.O.)
                    (on speakerphone)
              Where are you, babe!? You're on the
              floor in 45 minutes!>>>

Jake peeks over at his gold Rolex wristwatch.

                                                        (CONTINUED)

                         GINA(V.O.)
                      (on speakerphone)
                 >>>Get over here ASAP.

                           JAKE
                      I'm leaving now.

He hangs up and stares at the painting for a moment. He gives a deep
sigh, picks up his Porsche keys, and leaves.

4   **EXT. DOWNTOWN PITTSBURGH - NIGHT**

       It's raining. A super nice red Porsche speeds through downtown
       Pittsburgh. Pennsylvania license plate "JK D ICE."

5   **EXT. PITTSBURGH INTERSECTION - NIGHT**

       SENSEI YUMI, a Japanese man(early 70's) with an accent, walks the
       sidewalk, dressed in sensei attire. A staff sits on his shoulder,
       carrying a grocery bag on each end.

       Yumi crosses the street as Jake's Porsche speeds around the corner.
       Jake punches the brakes.

       *****************************SLOW MOTION****************************

       Yumi leaps high into the air as the car slides underneath him. A
       formidable distance forms between them.

       ***************************BACK TO NORMAL**************************

6   **INT. JAKE'S PORSCHE - NIGHT**

       Adrenaline rushes through Jake's veins. He exits the car>>>

7   **EXT. PITTSBURGH INTERSECTION - NIGHT**

       >>>and checks the Porsche for damages, then looks over>>>

       YUMI'S POSITION:

       >>>at Sensei Yumi, who is picking groceries off the street.

                           JAKE
                      (from a distance)
                 Hey!... Why don't you watch where
                 you're going next time!?

       Yumi cannot make out Jake's face, for it is dark.

                         SENSEI YUMI
                 Go in peace, my son. All is well.

       JAKE'S POSITION:

       Jake peeks over at his gold wristwatch, then back at Yumi. He gets
       back into his car and drives off, tires squealing.

8   INT. YUMI'S PLACE/MUSEUM ROOM - NIGHT

Sensei Yumi enters a museum-like room decorated with martial arts trophies and collectibles. He turns on the TV by hand. COMMENTATOR TY, an Asian man in his 50's, and COMMENTATOR DAVE, a white man in his 60's, comment on a martial arts competition underway.

                COMMENTATOR TY(TV)
        Daniels' instructor left him only after 2
        competitions. Vincent Harris currently fills
        the position, but we have yet to see any kind
        of professional interaction between the two.

Yumi inserts a VHS Tape into the VCR and presses record, then exits the room. We slowly slide into the TV screen.

                COMMENTATOR DAVE(TV)
        Every fighter present wants a shot at the
        national title held in Detroit 4 months
        from now, in addition to a record breaking
        $100,000 grand prize.
                (to Dave)
        Don't you wish they had that prize when
        we competed?

                COMMENTATOR DAVE(TV)
        Yeah, that woulda been nice.
                (to Audience)
        There are well over 80 fighters lined up on
        the floor. The best of luck to everyone.

9   INT. YUMI'S PLACE/DOJO - NIGHT

Sense Yumi goes through a course of gymnastics equipment, totally blindfolded. Station by station he performs the most breathtaking acrobatic moves. He lands the last station with one knee on the pad, does the sign of the cross, and prays.

10   INT. PITTSBURGH STADIUM/COMPETITION FLOOR - NIGHT (MONTAGE)

Round after round, Jake takes down his opponents flawlessly and without any mercy.

11   INT. PITTSBURGH STADIUM/COMPETITION FLOOR - NIGHT

COMMENTATOR'S POSITION:

                COMMENTATOR TY
        We are down to the last match for this
        evening. Jake "The Ice" Daniels and Bruce
        Wright, with Daniels being the favorite
        to win tonight's competition.

                COMMENTATOR DAVE
        That's right, but one thing we know is
        how quickly things can change in these
        tournaments.

                                        (CONTINUED)

>   COMMENTATOR TY
>   The match is just about to begin.
>   Let's go right to the action.

CENTER FLOOR:

Jake and BRUCE, a white man in his 20's, line up to fight.

>   PITTSBURGH REFEREE
>   Face each other... Bow... FIGHT!

With one merciless move, Jake takes him down so violently the medical
team rushes in.

>   JAKE
>   (arrogantly)
>   YEAHHHHHH! YEAHHHHHH! THAT IS HOW
>   YOU DO IT RIGHT THERE! YEAHHHHHH!

>   PITTSBURGH ANNOUNCER
>   (overhead speakers)
>   And our champion for this evening
>   is, Jake "The Ice" Daniels.

The crowd boos.

>   JAKE
>   BOO TO YOU, LOSERS!

12   **INT. PITTSBURGH STADIUM/COMPETITION FLOOR - NIGHT (LATER)**

TV REPORTER, a woman in her 30's, dressed very conservatively,
interviews Jake on live TV.

>   TV REPORTER
>   Is there anyone you'd like to thank
>   for tonight's victory?

>   JAKE
>   Yeah, 3 people. Me, myself, and I.

In the background, the first responders roll Bruce away on an
ambulance stretcher.

>   TV REPORTER
>   (dumbfounded)
>   Oh. You don't have anyone to thank?

>   JAKE
>   Besides the 3? No.

An awkward moment arises between them. She clears her throat.

>   TV REPORTER
>   Okay... Some would say your
>   fighting style is- how should I put
>   it? A little over the top, for lack
>   of some better words? Do you agree?

13   **INT. YUMI'S PLACE/MUSEUM ROOM - NIGHT**

Sensei Yumi watches Jake's live interview.

> JAKE(TV)
> I'm here to win, not whine.

> TV REPORTER(TV)
> Thank you for your time, Jake Daniels.
> Good luck with the rest of your competitions.

> JAKE(TV)
> I don't need luck, but thanks.

> SENSEI YUMI
>   (to himself)
> Jake "The Ice" Idiot!

He shuts off the TV and walks over to a monument that sits on a stand in the center of the room. It's covered by a black cloth. He places his hand on top of the monument, gives off a deep sorrowful sigh, and exits the room.

14   **INT. PITTSBURGH STADIUM/LOCKER ROOM - NIGHT**

Jake finishes dressing. GINA, a gorgeous, voluptuous blonde walks up to him with FOUR HIGH CLASS GIRLFRIENDS.

> GINA
> Good job, Babe!

Gina gives him a quick kiss.

> JAKE
> There's my sweet piece.

> GINA
> Me and my friends wanna go clubbing.
> Wanna come?

> JAKE
> But we already made plans!

> GINA
>   (confused)
> We did?

> JAKE
> Uhhhh... Yeah, we did.

> GINA
> Oh really!?

> JAKE
> Konia's Bistro- My birthday- Remember?

> GINA
> Oh yeah! Now that you mentioned it,
> I kinda remember something.

(CONTINUED)

                         JAKE
               And?

                         GINA
               And what?

                         JAKE
               Are we going to Konia's for my
               birthday, or what?

                         GINA
               Well, I already told my girlfriends I'd
               go clubbing with them. I don't want to
               disappoint them.

                         JAKE
               But it's alright to disappoint me.

                         GINA
               C'mon Jakey Poo! What's the big
               deal? We can go tomorrow.

                         JAKE
               Tomorrow I'm going to Lancaster for the
               next competition! I told you that too!

                         GINA
               So we'll go when you get back.

Jake realizes he's not getting anywhere.

                         JAKE
               Hey, if hanging out with your
               girlfriends is more important, then
               go hang out with your girlfriends.

                         GINA
               I knew you'd see it my way.

Moment of silence as Gina sticks out her hand.

                         JAKE
                    (confused)
               What?

                         GINA
               The club isn't free, you know. Duh!

Jake gives off a sigh, whips out a credit card, and gives it to her.
Without saying a word, she takes it and leaves.

                         JAKE
                    (to himself)
               You're welcome.

Jake closes the locker revealing CHORK, a rough looking, pony-tail,
Asian-American man in his 40's, dressed in a nice business suit.

                         JAKE
                    (frightened)
               What the...

                                                        (CONTINUED)

                        CHORK
              Well, hello Jake. Long time no see.

                        JAKE
              Chork! You scared the daylights
              outta me!

                        CHORK
              You should be scared. You should be very
              scared. The Boss is not happy with you,
              Jake. And you know why he's not happy?

                        JAKE
              I'm going to pay him, I swear!

                        CHORK
              You've been saying that for weeks, and
              frankly we're fed up with your excuses.
              The Boss has gotten this crazy idea-
              Oh, I don't know, that you might try to
              skip town on us. Is that crazy, Jake?

                        JAKE
              I would never do that! I've been really
              busy with my competitions, that's all.

                        CHORK
              Oh, I saw who you're busy with and I do
              have to congratulate you on your good taste.
              Goods like that must cost a fortune, eh?

                        JAKE
              My girl has nothing to do with this!

                        CHORK
              It has everything to do with it when you're
              throwing my boss' money on your woman.

CHECK DELIVERY MAN, an older man in his 60's, walks up to Jake with
a clipboard in his hand.

                        CHECK DELIVERY MAN
              Sign here.

Jake pulls a pen out of his duffle bag and signs.

                        CHECK DELIVERY MAN
              Thank you.

The man gives Jake an envelope and leaves.

                        CHORK
              What's this?

Chork pulls the envelope from Jake's hand and peeks inside.

                        CHORK
              Hey! That's not bad for one night.

                         JAKE
              I was gonna cash it and give it to
              him tomorrow.

                         CHORK
              There's no tomorrow, Jake. There's
              only now.

                         JAKE
              I don't have the money now.

Chork takes the pen from Jake and sees "JTID" etched in.

                         CHORK
              Nice pen you got here. Gold plated?

                         JAKE
              You can have it.

                         CHORK
              Well, that's really nice of you.

Chork takes the pen and slides it in the inner pocket of his suit.

                         CHORK
              Let's go for a ride, shall we?

Jake swallows hard with a panicked look on his face.

15   **EXT. NIGHT CLUB - NIGHT**

      It's raining. We see a nice black limousine pull in front of a
      luxurious night club, located in a run-down neighborhood. Chork and
      Jake get out.

16   **INT. NIGHT CLUB/DANCE FLOOR - NIGHT**

      Chork and Jake walk by the CLUBBERS.

                         CHORK
                    (to Jake)
              Hey! Check out that blonde over
              there. Pretty hot, huh?

      Jake looks over and sees GINA dancing dirty with some CLUB STRANGER.
      Jake is about to go to her, but Chork grabs him.

                         CHORK
              Business first, my friend.

      They walk over to a door guarded by BRUTE #1 and BRUTE #2. Both
      brutes move to the side, allowing them to pass.

17   **INT. NIGHT CLUB/STAIRS--->BOSS' OFFICE - NIGHT**

      A flickering florescent light shines the way as Jake and Chork walk
      down a set of poorly lit stairs. Muffled cheers and whistles are

heard as they approach the door at bottom. Chork presses a door bell. A narrow slit opens in the door, then closes, and BRUTE #3 opens the door. They go through revealing a brutal martial arts fight is currently underway inside a professional boxing ring. Chork and Jake walk past the ring and walk to another door, guarded by BRUTE #4.

18   **INT. NIGHT CLUB/BASEMENT/BOSS' OFFICE - NIGHT**

BOSS, an Asian man in his 60's, dressed in a nice Armani suit, sits behind a nice luxurious desk. Two huge piranha filled aquariums fill both sides of the entrance. One on left, one on right, with a glass tube connecting both sides.

Chork walks in, followed by Jake.

                    CHORK
              (to Boss)
         Look who decided to drop by.

                    BOSS
              (nicely)
         Well, if it ain't Jake "The Not So
         Nice" Daniels.
              (rudely)
         WHERE'S MY MONEY, YOU LITTLE
         BACKSTREET PUNK?

A panicked look forms on Jake's face.

                    JAKE
              (jittery voice)
         I was gonna give you a part of it
         first thing in the morning.

                    BOSS
         THERE IS NO MORNING, JAKE. THERE'S
         ONLY NOW.

                    CHORK
         Hey! That's what I told'm.

                    BOSS
              (to Chork)
         I'm sorry. Was I talking to you?

Chork stops talking.

                    BOSS
              (to Jake)
         I don't think you fully grasp the situation
         we find ourselves in. When you tell a man
         you're going to pay him, you pay him. It's
         as simple as that. If it were just between
         you and me, sure, I could pull a few strings
         in your favor, but this is not between you
         and me. There are bosses above me I got
         to answer to. What do I tell them when they
         start asking questions, huh Jake? Tell me?
         What do I tell them?

                                                          (CONTINUED)

                         JAKE
                    I was--

                         BOSS
                    I'm not finished!

Jake listens. An alarm goes off on Boss' smartphone. Boss gets up
from his desk and heads over to the fridge.

                         BOSS
                    Take me for example. I am an honest man.
                    I do not cheat anyone. I do not kill>>>

He puts on a pair of thick rubber gloves.

                         BOSS
                    >>>anyone. I do not take anything that
                    does not belong to me, and I pay all my
                    debts in full. I live by my own Golden>>>

He pulls out of the fridge a big piece of meat.

                         BOSS
                    >>>Rule, "Treat others as you would like to
                    be treated." Especially your enemies, Jake.
                    Especially your enemies! You know what
                    happens to me if I do not pay my debts?

Boss throws the fish into the aquarium. The piranhas devour the meat
like it was nothing.

                         BOSS
                    Get the picture?

He takes off the gloves and makes it back to the desk.

                         JAKE
                    I was going to cash the check from
                    tonight's game and give it to you.

                         BOSS
                    What check?

Chork hands Boss the envelope. Boss pulls the check out.

                         BOSS
                    This is 3K. I cannot wipe my rear
                    with this insulting piece of paper.

                         JAKE
                    How about my Rolex?

Jake shows him the watch.

                         BOSS
                    We gave you cash, we want cash.

                         JAKE
                    I don't have the money right now, but give
                    me 4 more weeks. All the winnings from
                    the competitions I'll turn over to you.

                                                    (CONTINUED)

                         BOSS
          Even if you win every competition, that's
          still not enough to settle your debt.
          How do you plan on getting the rest?

Jake swallows with doubt.

                         JAKE
          I don't know. I'll get a real job.

                         BOSS
                (to Chork)
          He's gonna get a real job.
                (to Jake)
          That's cute. Very cute. You have a
          better chance selling cookies to street
          beggars, if you ask me.

Boss gets out of his chair and walks around for a tad.

                         BOSS
          I don't know what to do with you,
          Jake. If it were anyone else in your
          shoes, we woulda had them whacked by now.
          But... I like you. Not sure why I like
          you, but I do.

Boss sits back at his desk and looks over the check.

                         BOSS
                (to Chork)
          This look good to you?

                         CHORK
          I was there when they gave it to him.

Boss ponders for a moment.

                         BOSS
          Tell you what I'll do, Jake. I'll make
          you an offer you will not refuse, and
          I do mean "will not" refuse. What do
          you say to that?

                         JAKE
          Sure.

                         BOSS
          This check and your watch buys you 4
          weeks. Sign it over to me and you'll
          still owe us 50K. Sound good to you?

Jake nods in approval.

                         BOSS
          I want my money in 4 weeks. 4 weeks is
          all you get. This is your last chance,
          Jake. 4 weeks from today, or you're
          going to live up to your name, if you
          know what I mean.

                        CHORK
                  (to Jake)
            Get it? Jake "The Ice." You know,
            "Ice." Get it?

                        BOSS
                  (to Chork)
            I thought I told you to shut up!?
                  (to Jake)
            This is not fun and games, Jake. This is
            serious business. If you do not have the
            cash by then, you'll be digging your own
            grave. Capisce?

Jake nods.

                        BOSS
            Good... Sign it!

Boss slides the check to Jake.

                        JAKE
            Got a pen?

                        CHORK
                  (to Jake)
            Here, use mine. It's gold plated.

Chork hands Jake the same gold pen that Jake gave him. Jake signs it,
takes off his watch, places the watch on top of the check, and slides
them over to Boss. Boss takes the check and verifies the signature.

                        BOSS
            Good. Now get out of my sight.

Jake gets up and walks toward the door. He turns around.

                        JAKE
            Could someone give me a ride back?

Boss and Chork look at each other and laugh.

                        BOSS
                  (to Chork)
            Did he just say what I thought he said?

                        CHORK
            He did!

Laughs continue.

                        BOSS
                  (to Chork)
            Just listen to this guy.

Laughs get harder.

19   **EXT. NIGHT CLUB/BACK ALLEY - NIGHT**

It's raining. Brute #1 and Brute #2 throw Jake out of the club
through a back-alley door. Jake trips and falls to the floor. He's
roughed up pretty good.

                    BRUTE #1(O.S.)
                (as they leave)
            Spoiled rich kids.

                    BRUTE #2(O.S.)
                (girly voice)
            My daddy buys me everything!

Jake wipes the blood off his lip.

20   **INT. RITZY HIGH-RISE/ELEVATOR - NIGHT**

Drenched, Jake rides the elevator with ELEVATOR ATTENDANT, a female
in her 50's. He wipes his bloody lip with his hand.

                    ELEVATOR ATTENDANT
            Tissue, Sir?

Jake takes the tissue and sets it on his lip.

                    JAKE
            Thanks.

21   **INT. RITZY HIGH-RISE/HALLWAY - NIGHT**

Elevator opens. Jake walks down the hallway of his apartment complex
and begins to cough. MIKEY, an overweight, 40-year-old white man,
with a New York accent, turns the corner.

                    MIKEY
            Hey Jakey, my bro! Congrats on the
            big win.

Mikey acts as if he's karate chopping Jake.

                    JAKE
            Thanks, Mikey.

Jake's coughs get harder.

                    MIKEY
            Ya a'right?

                    JAKE
            Yeah-yeah, I'm good.

                    MIKEY
            Ya sure, cuz you ain't look'n good?

Jake slides his card key into the door and opens it.

                    JAKE
            I'm sure-I'm sure! Thanks for asking.

22   **INT. RITZY HIGH-RISE/JAKE'S APARTMENT - NIGHT**

Jake enters his apartment coughing, but after a moment the coughs subside. He turns on the light. The apartment is cold, empty, and void of life.

He passes by his newly painted creation and stares at it for a moment. An expression of distaste forms on his face. He picks up a paint brush and with the back end, pokes two holes through the painting. We see the brush exit the back.

                    JAKE
          Blind is what you are.

He leaves. We circle around to reveal a modern art painting of a psychotic twisted man, with holes in the eyes.

23   **INT. RITZY HIGH-RISE/JAKE'S BEDROOM - NIGHT**

Weary, Jake lays on the bed staring up at the ceiling.

DIGITAL CLOCK: BEEP-BEEP!

Jake looks over at the desk clock. It's exactly 12:00am.

                    JAKE
               (softly to himself)
          Happy Birthday.

He gives a sigh and goes to sleep.

Lightning enters through the window, followed by thunder.

VOCAL FAITH SONG BEGINS...

24   **EXT. PORSCHE TRAVELING MONTAGE - DAY**

It's raining. We see an assortment of shots where Jake's Porsche travels through Pennsylvania.

25   **EXT. FREEWAY - DUSK**

It's raining heavily. We slide over to the side of the freeway to see a warning sign.

CAUTION ROAD SIGN: "HEAVY FLOODING AHEAD - FOLLOW DETOUR"

Jake's Porsche passes in the background.

26   **INT. JAKE'S PORSCHE - DUSK (TRAVELING)**

                    JAKE
               (sarcastic tone)
          I can't take all this good luck.

27   **EXT. COUNTRY ROAD - DUSK**

Jake's Porsche passes by a road sign.

ROAD SIGN: "Mt. Joy - 30 Miles"

28   **EXT. COUNTRY BRIDGE - NIGHT**

ROAD SIGN: "WATER OVER BRIDGE - CROSS WITH CAUTION"

GRACIE Jacobs, an innocent and very attractive, 19-year-old Amish girl, along with her brother, ABE, an Amish man in his 20's, cross a bridge in a covered buggy.

A bright light-post lights up the bridge. They slowly make their way across, wheels buried halfway in water.

VOCAL FAITH SONG ENDS.

29   **INT. JAKE'S PORSCHE - NIGHT (TRAVELING)**

Jake tries to make a phone call, but can't get a signal.

                    JAKE
            C'mon work!

30   **EXT. COUNTRY BRIDGE - NIGHT**

The car and buggy come within viewing range of one another.

*****************************SLOW MOTION****************************

Jake and Gracie catch a glimpse of each other as they pass.

***************************BACK TO NORMAL**************************

Emotions overwhelm them both.

                    GRACIE
                 (to Abe)
            He needs to slow down.

31   **INT. JAKE'S PORSCHE - NIGHT (TRAVELING)**

Jake, mesmerized by Gracie's beauty, doesn't pay attention to what lies ahead.

                    JAKE
            Oh wow!

32   **INT. JACOBS' BUGGY - NIGHT (TRAVELING)**

Gracie looks back with concern.

                    GRACIE
            He's not slowing down, Abe!

33   **INT. JAKE'S PORSCHE - NIGHT (TRAVELING)**

Jake continues to be mesmerized.

                         JAKE
                 (different intonation)
            Wow-oh-wow!

34   **EXT. COUNTRY BRIDGE - NIGHT**

Jake's Porsche passes the "WATER OVER BRIDGE" road sign. The car hits
the water and spins, losing control. The car hits a tree ricocheting
it next to the river's edge.

35   **INT. JACOBS' BUGGY - NIGHT (TRAVELING)**

Gracie and Abe witness the accident.

                        GRACIE
                 TURN AROUND!

Abe remains motionless.

                        GRACIE
                 HE NEEDS OUR HELP, ABE!

Abe continues forward. Immediately, Gracie jumps out and runs toward
the bridge. Abe pulls on the driving strap.

                         ABE
                    (to horse)
              Whoaaaaaa!

The buggy comes to a stop.

36   **INT. JAKE'S PORSCHE - NIGHT**

The water level rises quickly as Jake is passed out cold.

37   **EXT. COUNTRY BRIDGE - NIGHT**

Gracie runs into the waist high water. She pulls the door handle,
but it's jammed shut. She goes underwater; losing the head covering,
finds a larger rock, and breaks the window. She unbuckles the
seatbelt and tries to pull Jake out. The car inches its way deeper
into the river.

                        GRACIE
                 HELP ME, ABE! HELP ME!

At the last second, Abe grabs them both. Immediately the car is
pulled into the rushing water and floats away.

38   **INT. JACOBS' HOUSE/ABE'S BEDROOM - DAY**

JAKE'S POV:

The screen is completely black.

>   GRACIE (O.S.)
>   I think he is coming around.

Jake opens his eyes and sees only blurriness until he finally focuses
on beautiful Gracie.

GRACIE & JAKE'S POSITION:

>   JAKE
>   Am I in heaven?

>   GRACIE
>   No, but you came this close.

She shows him with her fingers.

>   JAKE
>   I have to be, because you are the
>   prettiest angel I have ever seen
>   in my life.

Gracie chuckles as she looks over at Abe, who is two steps away.

>   GRACIE
>   (to Abe)
>   I like him. He is funny.
>   (to Jake)
>   What is your name?

>   JAKE
>   (confused)
>   Name?

Jake looks around in confusion.

>   GRACIE
>   You know, the name your parents
>   gave you.

>   JAKE
>   (thinking)
>   My name...

Jake takes a deep breath and slowly lets it out.

>   JAKE
>   I don't know my name.

>   GRACIE
>   You do not know your name?

He shakes his head.

>   JAKE
>   I can't remember.

(CONTINUED)

                         GRACIE
          Do you know how you got here?

                         JAKE
          No.

                         GRACIE
          You hit a tree with your car and went
          "sleepy-bye." My brother and I rescued you.

                         JAKE
          I guess that would explain the pain
          in my leg.

Gracie looks over at Abe.

                         GRACIE
              (to Abe)
          He may have amnesia.

Abe nods.

                         ABE
          Yes.

                         JAKE
          I should get up.

                         GRACIE ABE
          No!!! No!!!

Jake looks under the sheets.

                         GRACIE
          Your clothes are drying, sorry.

ELLA, a girl in her 20's, Gracie's older sister, enters the bedroom.

                         ELLA
          Father wants to talk to you.

                         GRACIE
          To me?

                         ELLA
          To both of you.

Gracie looks over at Abe with concern.

39   **INT. JACOBS' HOUSE/KITCHEN - DAY**

MRS. JACOBS, an Amish woman in her 40's, Gracie's mother, prepares
something in the kitchen. MR. JACOBS, an Amish man also in his 40's,
Gracie's father, enters limping on a cane and takes a seat at the
kitchen table. She coughs lightly.

                         MR. JACOBS
          Are you well, Mrs. Jacobs?

                                                            (CONTINUED)

                          MRS. JACOBS
                    I am nervous about the wedding
                    tomorrow. Would you like some tea?

                          MR. JACOBS
                    Yes, thank you.

Mr. Jacobs sticks a newspaper in his face; "*Amish Times*." Gracie
and Abe enter.

                          GRACIE
                    You wanted to see us, Father?

                          MR. JACOBS
                    Yes... Have a seat.

They take a seat at the kitchen table. Gracie glances over at her
mother. Mrs. Jacobs shakes her head. Moment of silence as Mr. Jacobs
looks over the newspaper.

                          MR. JACOBS
                    Did you finish plowing the South
                    Field, Abe?

Mr. Jacobs stares into the newspapers as they talk.

                          ABE
                    No, Father. I will try to finish it today
                    and hopefully start on the North tomorrow.

                          MR. JACOBS
                    Very good.

Moment of awkward silence.

                          MR. JACOBS
                    And how is our guest? Comfy, I hope.

Abe nods to Gracie.

                          GRACIE
                    I think he has amnesia.

                          MR. JACOBS
                    And how do you know? Are you a doctor?

                          GRACIE
                    He does not remember a thing, not
                    even his name.

Mr. Jacobs never makes eye contact with them, but stays
focused on the paper.

                          MR. JACOBS
                    Amnesia, huh?

                          GRACIE
                    Yes, Father.

Gracie looks over at Abe. Abe shakes his head.

(CONTINUED)

>   GRACIE
>   I should take him--

Mr. Jacobs puts down the paper and looks directly at her.

>   MR. JACOBS
>   What is this, "I?"

Gracie clears her throat.

>   GRACIE
>   It does not have to be me. I mean,
>   Abe could do it.

Mrs. Jacobs sets the cup of tea in front of Mr. Jacobs and leaves.

>   MR. JACOBS
>   Thank you, Mrs. Jacobs.

Mr. Jacobs takes a sip of the tea and buries himself in the paper.

>   GRACIE
>   So?

>   MR. JACOBS
>   What, "so?"

>   GRACIE
>   May Abe take him?

>   MR. JACOBS
>   I'm afraid Abe is very busy today.

An awkward moment of silence forms between them.

40   **EXT. JACOBS' FARM - DAY**

Abe helps Jake(dressed in his city clothes) get into the back of the
carriage filled with hay. Gracie and Mr. Jacobs are a few steps away.
BARK, a German Shepherd dog, barks like crazy.

>   MR. JACOBS
>   (to Bark)
>   THAT'S ENOUGH, BARK!

Bark goes inside the dog house, lays down, and whines.

>   MR. JACOBS
>   (to Gracie)
>   Do not forget what I said.

>   GRACIE
>   "Drop the English man and come right
>   back; the Yoder's need the carriage."

>   MR. JACOBS
>   Very good.

Mr. Jacobs gives Gracie a kiss on the forehead.

(CONTINUED)

                         MR. JACOBS
                    God be with you.

                         GRACIE
                    And with you, Father.

Gracie gets into the carriage.

                         GRACIE
                         (to horse)
                    Hyaaaaaa!

The carriage rolls away.

                         MR. JACOBS
                    That lad reminds me of someone.

                         ABE
                    Who, Father?

Mr. Jacobs ponders for a moment.

                         MR. JACOBS
                    Someone I used to know.

They walk toward the barn.

41   **EXT. COUNTRY ROAD/CARRIAGE - DAY (TRAVELING)**

Gracie drives the carriage. Jake lays flat in the back.

                         JAKE
                    You never told me your name.

Gracie hesitates for a moment, but gives in.

                         GRACIE
                         (softly)
                    Gracie.

She swallows with emotion.

                         JAKE
                    I'm sorry, what was that? I didn't
                    hear you?

She clears her throat and turns her face toward him.

                         GRACIE
                    Gracie, that is my name. Gracie Jacobs.

                         JAKE
                    That's a nice name.

                         GRACIE
                    Thank you.

Moment of silence forms between them.

                       JAKE
What about your brother? I'm assuming
he's your brother, yes?

                       GRACIE
He is my brother. Abe is his name.

                       JAKE
He does not say much, does he?

                       GRACIE
He is shy talking with new people.

                       JAKE
I see.

Moment of silence.

                       JAKE
Don't you want to know my name?

                       GRACIE
         (with subtle laughter)
You do not remember... remember?

Jake laughs lightly with her.

                       JAKE
You're right. That wasn't a very
smart question on my part. Then why
don't you pick out a name for me?

                       GRACIE
You want me to pick a name for you?

                       JAKE
I do.

                       GRACIE
I am sorry, but I cannot.

                       JAKE
Why not?

                       GRACIE
Because I cannot.

                       JAKE
You can't or you won't?

                       GRACIE
Both.

Moment of silence as Jake ponders.

                       JAKE
         (to himself)
I think I'll just call myself Harry, or
maybe Buck... How about Guber? Yeah, that's
a good name! Guber. Hey Guber! Come over
here, Guber! It's got a nice ring to it.

                        GRACIE
            None of those names fit you.

                        JAKE
            They don't?

                        GRACIE
            No.

                        JAKE
            Then what name fits me?

Gracie ponders for a tad.

                        GRACIE
            You have the resemblance of an Isaac.

                        JAKE
            You think so?

                        GRACIE
            It is only my opinion. It matters
            not, what I think.

                        JAKE
            It matters to me, Gracie.

Moment of silence.

                        JAKE
            Then that's my name. Isaac... Isaac
            uhhhhhhh>>>

He sees the name "Abrams" on the side of a Mailbox.

                        JAKE
            >>>hhhhh, Abrams. Isaac Abrams.
            That's my name.

Gracie gives off a slight chuckle.

                        GRACIE
            You snagged it off the mailbox.

                        JAKE
            How do you know that?

                        GRACIE
            Because you did. I am certain of it.

                        JAKE
            Yes, but how do you know for sure?

                        GRACIE
            I am sure. Just admit it!

                        JAKE
            Okay, fine, I give up. You got me...
            but I almost had you there.

                        GRACIE
            You certainly did not!

42   **EXT. MT. JOY MEDICAL CLINIC - DAY**

The carriage pulls in front of the Mt. Joy Medical Clinic.

                    GRACIE
               (to horse)
          Whoaaaaaa!
               (to Jake)
          We have arrived.

Jake tries to get out, but has a hard time.

                    GRACIE
          Should I get someone to help you?

                    JAKE
          No-no, I got it.

He gets out of the carriage bed and circles around to the front,
holding onto the carriage for support. They look at each other for
a moment, neither knowing what to say. Gracie clears her throat and
looks the other way.

                    JAKE
          Thanks for saving my life, and
          taking such good care of me.

                    GRACIE
          You do not need to thank me, Isaac.
          I am certain you would have done
          the same for me.

Moment of silence.

                    JAKE
               (pointing)
          Is this the place?

                    GRACIE
          Yes. Dr. Collins is of the English.
          He takes good care of us.

                    JAKE
          Okay, then I'd better get myself
          checked out, huh?

                    GRACIE
          I wish I could stay, but--

                    JAKE
          Yes, I overheard your father talking.
          I appreciate all that you've done
          for me, Gracie.
               (with emotions)
          Will I see you again?

Gracie gives a light sigh.

                    GRACIE
          Probably not.

(CONTINUED)

Jake puts out his hand for a handshake.

> JAKE
> Goodbye, Gracie. It was nice
> getting to know you.

Gracie stares at his hand.

> JAKE
> I just want to shake your hand.

She looks around hesitantly, shakes his hand, and quickly pulls back
at the end.

> GRACIE
> May God be with you, Isaac.
>   (to horse)
> Hyaaaaaaaaaaa!

The carriage strolls away slowly.

GRACIE'S POSITION:

After a moment, Gracie gazes back at Jake.

JAKE'S POSITION:

Jake notices her looking back and waves to her. He takes a step
toward the clinic and falls to the ground.

GRACIE'S POSITION:

Gracie sees Jake fall.

> GRACIE
> ISAAC!!!

She stops the horse and runs toward him.

> GRACIE
> ISAAC!!!

JAKE'S POSITION:

Gracie approaches Jake in a rush.

> GRACIE
> I knew I should have gotten someone
> to help you. I knew it!

> JAKE
> It's okay, Gracie. I'm fine.
> Nothing happened.

> GRACIE
> I need to park the carriage. Do not move.

43   **INT. MT. JOY MEDICAL CLINIC - DAY**

Jake lays on the clinic bed, while Gracie sits on the chair beside
him. DR. COLLINS, a white man in his 60's, dressed in a white lab
coat, holds a notepad.

                    DR. COLLINS
              By what you've told me, he's lucky
              to be alive. Only a sprained ankle
              and a few bruises.

                    GRACIE
              What about his memory loss?

                    DR. COLLINS
              Well, I'm not sure what to say about
              that. Amnesia can last days, months,
              and sometimes even years. It's hard
              to say when, or for that matter, if
              he's gonna get it back.

                    JAKE
              Are you saying, I might never know
              who I am?

                    DR. COLLINS
              There's a possibility of that, yes-
              but if worse comes to worse, you
              could always relearn who you were.

                    JAKE
              How do I do that? I don't even know
              where I live?

                    DR. COLLINS
                  (to Jake)
              Didn't you have any I.D. on you?

Jake looks over at Gracie.

                    GRACIE
              What is I.D.?

                    DR. COLLINS
              Identification of some sort.

                    GRACIE
                  (to Doctor)
              He did not have anything on him.
              Perhaps in the car.

                    DR. COLLINS
              I'd head over to the Sheriff as soon as
              possible and let him know your situation.
              He's the only one who can help you.

                    GRACIE
              Yes, we will do as you say.

(CONTINUED)

> DR. COLLINS
> I'm gonna give you these crutches,
> Isaac. Please take good care of
> them, we reuse things around here.

Gracie takes the crutches from Dr. Collins.

> JAKE
> I will.

Dr. Collins is just about to leave.

> DR. COLLINS
> Oh, there is one other thing I wanted to
> say. People who suffer from amnesia, many
> times suffer from a personality change.

> JAKE
> Personality change?

> DR. COLLINS
> I'm not saying this happened to
> you, I'm saying it's a possibility.

> JAKE
> Why is that?

> DR. COLLINS
> Our past makes us who we are as a
> person. Without knowing our past,
> we may become a different person.

A deep thought forms on Jake's face.

44   **EXT. MT. JOY POLICE STATION - DAY**

Gracie stops the carriage in front of the police station.

> GRACIE
> (to horse)
> Whoaaaaaa!

Jake tries to get out of the carriage by himself.

> GRACIE
> (to Jake)
> Do not move. I will help you.

She goes to the back and helps him get off, then hands him
the crutches.

> JAKE
> Thank you for showing me such
> kindness, Gracie.

Gracie blushes with delight and gives him a nod. They slowly
make their way to the front of the carriage.

> JAKE
> Will your Father be angry with you
> for returning so late?

> GRACIE
> I will tell him the truth and
> whatever happens, happens.

Gracie climbs into the driver's seat of the carriage.

> GRACIE
> I pray all goes well with you, Isaac, and
> you return safely to your home.

> JAKE
> (with slight emotion)
> Any chance I could see you again?

Gracie gives a sigh and ponders for a tad.

> GRACIE
> Only if the Lord wills. Good-bye, Isaac.
> (to horse)
> Hyaaaaaa!

With sadness, Jake observes the carriage slowly pulling away.

45   **INT. MT. JOY POLICE STATION - DAY**

KLOEY, a lady in her 50's with a southern accent, types on a classic
typewriter. BETSY, a lady in her 40's, walks in from the back.

> BETSY
> Alright, Kloey. I'm taking off. Night
> shifts suck the life outta me. I don't
> know how you can do 2 jobs. I can
> barely handle this one.

> KLOEY
> I enjoy being in between all those
> books. Besides it's only every
> other Saturday.

> BETSY
> Ahhhhhh... I'll see you tomorrow.

> KLOEY
> Later, Betsy.

Betsy leaves. A tad later, JAKE crutches clumsily through the door.

> KLOEY
> How may I help you, young man?

> JAKE
> My car is at the bottom of a river
> and I need someone to get it out.

(CONTINUED)

                         KLOEY
          Well that's not good! How did your
          car end up at the bottom of a river?

                         JAKE
          That's a very good question. I just came
          from the doctor down the street and he
          says I've got amnesia. I can't remember
          anything since this morning, that's why
          I need to get to my car and hopefully find
          something to get me home.

                         KLOEY
               (with compassion)
          Oh, poor thing. I hope you're alright.

                         JAKE
          The doctor said I'll be fine. Just
          gotta use these crutches for a time.

                         KLOEY
          That's good to hear. Why don't you
          have a seat. The Sheriff should be
          arriving any time now.

                         JAKE
          Okay.

Jake crutches over to the seats.

46   **EXT. JACOBS' FARM - DAY**

A police car pulls into the driveway of Gracie's home.

POLICE CAR: HONK-HONK!!!

47   **INT. JACOBS' HOUSE/LIVING ROOM - DAY**

Gracie hears the horn and curiously peeks out the window.

48   **EXT. JACOBS' FARM - DAY**

Mr. Jacobs comes out of the barn walking on a cane for support.
SHERIFF PHIL, a black man in his 40's, gets out and walks over to
Mr. Jacobs. Bark, the dog, barks like crazy.

                         MR. JACOBS
          ENOUGH, BARK!

Bark stops, whines, and sits on the floor saddened.

                         SHERIFF PHIL
          Good afternoon, Mr. Jacobs.

                         MR. JACOBS
          What brings you here, Sheriff?

They both walk towards each other until they meet.

                    SHERIFF PHIL
          I have a young man at the station who
          says Gracie and Abe rescued him last
          night. I'm hoping they could provide
          me with the whereabouts of the accident.

                    MR. JACOBS
          Abe is out plowing, but you may chat
          with Gracie, if you like.

                    SHERIFF PHIL
          That would be great.

49   **EXT. JACOBS' HOUSE/PORCH - DAY**

Sheriff Phil and Gracie are on the porch.

                    SHERIFF PHIL
          Anything else you'd like to add?

                    GRACIE
          That is everything. Do you know
          what will happen to him?

                    SHERIFF PHIL
          Once we pull out the car, everything
          should take care of itself. At least
          that's what we hope.

                    GRACIE
          Where is he living?

                    SHERIFF PHIL
          We've made arrangements with the
          local motel to let him stay there
          for a week or two.

                    GRACIE
          And after that?

                    SHERIFF PHIL
          I don't know. We'll have to see
          how it all plays out.

Sheriff Phil gets up to leave. Gracie stands with him.

                    SHERIFF PHIL
          I appreciate your help, Gracie.

                    GRACIE
          You are welcome, Sheriff. Does he
          have anything to eat?

He turns toward her.

                    SHERIFF PHIL
          Oh, I haven't really thought
          about that! I guess I'll ask my
          wife to whip him up something.

                         GRACIE
          Do you mind waiting a few minutes? I
          would like to give him a little something.

                         SHERIFF PHIL
                    (with surprise)
          Oh, sure. That's very kind of you.

50   **INT. MT. JOY MOTEL/JAKE'S ROOM - NIGHT**

Jake lays on the bed, gazing up at the ceiling.

MOTEL DOOR: KNOCK-KNOCK!

He gets on the side of the bed, grabs the crutches, and makes his way
to the door.

51   **EXT. MT. JOY MOTEL/JAKE'S ROOM - NIGHT**

Sheriff Phil stands by the motel door as Jake opens it.

                         SHERIFF PHIL
          Apologies for coming so late. For you.

Sheriff Phil hands Jake a bag.

                         JAKE
          What's this?

                         SHERIFF PHIL
          Gracie Jacobs packed you some food.

                         JAKE
          Well, that was nice of her!

                         SHERIFF PHIL
          Too nice, if you ask me.

                         JAKE
          "Too nice?"

                         SHERIFF PHIL
          Amish don't take well to outsiders.
          I was surprised when she offered.

                         JAKE
          Gracie has to be the nicest, kindest,
          prettiest girl I have ever met in my life.

Moment of silence as Sheriff Phil mulls over Jake's words.

                         SHERIFF PHIL
          Oh, Isaac, I hate to break it to you,
          but they don't mix with you and I.
          I've been sheriff in this town for over
          a decade, one thing I can say with
          certainty; they don't socialize outside
          their community, unless its business.
          Strictly business and nothing more.

(CONTINUED)

CONTINUED: 32.

                    JAKE
          Then why did she pack me this food?

                    SHERIFF PHIL
          I don't know, maybe she felt sorry for
          you, but it's definitely one in the
          books for me.

                    JAKE
          Did you get the info you needed?

                    SHERIFF PHIL
          I did. We're looking for a red sports
          car. Unfortunately, we can't get to
          it until the river returns to normal.

                    JAKE
          How long will that take?

                    SHERIFF PHIL
          If there's no more rain, I say about a
          week, maybe two, but finding your car is a
          whole other matter. The currents are strong
          here. The car could be anywhere downriver.

                    JAKE
          So I'm guessing I might be here
          for a while?

                    SHERIFF PHIL
          I'm sorry, Isaac. Things are what they
          are. Okay, I'm gonna head out. My wife
          and kids haven't seen me all day long.

Sheriff Phil makes his way to the car.

                    SHERIFF PHIL
          You need anything, call me. You got
          my number, right?

                    JAKE
          Yes. Kloey gave it to me.

                    SHERIFF PHIL
          Good. We'll talk more tomorrow.

Sheriff Phil gets in the police car and drives away.

52   **INT. MT. JOY MOTEL/JAKE'S ROOM - NIGHT**

Jake sits at the table. He opens the bag and pulls out the food and
lastly pulls out a Bible. He opens it to discover it's none other
than Gracie's Bible. He flips through it and a note falls out. He
opens the note and reads it.

                    GRACIE(V.O.)
               (note reads)
          *Hello, Isaac. Hope all is well. Sheriff
          Phil told me you were in need of food so*
               (MORE)

                                        (CONTINUED)

> GRACIE(V.O./cont'd)
> (note reads)
> *I packed you something. I hope you find*
> *it to your liking. I understand you will*
> *be staying for a little while. I am lending*
> *you my Bible to keep you occupied during*
> *your stay. Give it to Sheriff Phil when*
> *you leave. My favorite book is John.*
>
> *God Bless You, Isaac.*
>
> *Gracie.*

He takes the Bible, makes his way to the bed and starts
flipping through.

> JAKE
> John... John... Here it is.

He lays down on the bed and begins to read.

> JAKE(V.O.)
> (John 1:1-5(KJV))
> *(1) In the beginning was the Word, and*
> *the Word was with God, and the Word was*
> *God. (2) The same was in the beginning*
> *with God. (3) All things were made by him;*
> *and without him was not any thing made*
> *that was made. (4) In him was life;*
> *and the life was the light of men.*
> *(5) And the light shineth in darkness;*
> *and the darkness comprehended it not.*

53   **INT. BILLY'S BAR - DAY**

BULL, an overweight white man in his lower 30's, along with BULL'S
2 FRIENDS, also in their low 30's, are completely wasted. They chug
down the last of their beers.

> BULL
> Ahhhhhh! Now let's have some fun.

54   **EXT. MT. JOY/GENERAL STORE - DAY**

SAMUEL'S POSITION:

SAMUEL, an Amish man in his early 20's, exits the General Store with
a heavy box and loads it into the carriage. He proceeds to the front
of the carriage and prepares the horse. Samuel's sister,
SARAH(mid-teens), sits on the carriage seat.

BULL'S POSITION:

Bull, along with Bull's 2 Friends exit Billy's Bar, which is adjacent
to the General Store.

> BULL
> (to himself)
> Well, lookie what we got here!

                                                          (CONTINUED)

SAMUEL'S POSITION:

Bull walks up to Sarah.

>   BULL
> What's your name, pretty Chiquita?

She doesn't respond, but ignores him completely.

>   SAMUEL
>   (with rebuke)
> Leave my sister alone.

>   BULL
> Just chill, I only wanna talk to her.

>   SAMUEL
> Leave her alone, you troublemaker!

>   BULL
> Troublemaker! You called me a "troublemaker?"

>   SAMUEL
> I call you troublemaker, because you are a
> troublemaker. Everyone in this town knows it.

>   BULL
> Well then, I'll just have to live
> up to my reputation, won't I?

Bull pulls Sarah out of the carriage by force.

>   SARAH
> HELP ME, SAMUEL! HELP ME!

Bull's two friends quickly hold Samuel down.

55   **INT. MT. JOY MOTEL/JAKE'S ROOM - DAY**

Jake's on the bed sleeping. Gracie's Bible lays across his chest.
Sarah's screams awaken him.

56   **EXT. MT. JOY - DAY**

Sarah tries to break loose from Bull's grip.

>   SARAH
> SOMEONE HELP ME!

He tries to kiss her. She slaps him.

>   BULL
> Playing hard to get, huh? I like it!

>   JAKE(O.S.)
> YO LARD-MAN!

Bull looks over and sees Jake on crutches.

(CONTINUED)

                         JAKE
              What is your fat problem!?

Bull is in utter shock.

                         BULL
              What you call me?

                         JAKE
              Leave her alone, you giant tub of
              lard! She's done nothing to you!

Bull lets go of Sarah.

                         BULL
              I know you ain't talking to me,
              buddy old pal!

Bull's friends let go of Samuel. Sarah runs into her brother's arms.

                         JAKE
              Firstly, I'm not your buddy, and
              neither your pal. Secondly, you're
              the only tub of lard I see, but if
              you see another, kindly let me know.

                         BULL
              How 'bout I kindly make a knuckle
              sandwich outta you!?

                         JAKE
              I'm right here, big boy. What's
              stopping you?

Bull tries to beat-up Jake, but Jake deflects every blow using only
his crutches.

                         BULL
              That's it! No more Mr. Nice Guy.

Full of rage, Bull rushes towards Jake.

                         JAKE
              Watch your step.

Jake throws one crutch toward Bull's legs, causing Bull to trip. He
hits the ground hard, landing just a few inches away from Jake.

POLICE SIREN: EEEUUUUU-EEEUUUUU!

A Mt. Joy police car pulls near them. Bull's friends scatter.
Sheriff Phil gets out.

                         SHERIFF PHIL
              What's going on here?

                         SAMUEL
              This vagabond acted shamefully
              toward my sister. This brave
              young man stopped him.

                                                          (CONTINUED)

                         SHERIFF PHIL
                    (to Jake)
               For not remembering anything, you
               sure can handle yourself.

Bull groans as he wakes up.

                         SHERIFF PHIL
               Well now, Bull, you'll have to shake
               off that booze in jail, won't you?

Sheriff Phil cuffs him and pulls him off the floor.

                         SHERIFF PHIL
               How about two days this time? That
               will clear you right up.

Bull groans as he's taken away. Sarah picks up Jake's crutch.

                         SARAH
               Your stick.

Jake takes it.

                         SAMUEL
               I am greatly indebted to you. What
               is your name?

                         JAKE
               Isaac.

                         SAMUEL
               I am Samuel, and this is my sister,
               Sarah. You are not a familiar face.

                         JAKE
               Yeah, I'm just passing through.

                         SAMUEL
               How long will you be staying?

                         JAKE
               As of right now, a week, maybe two.
               I'm not really sure.

                         SAMUEL
               Is there any way I can recompense
               you for your good deed?

                         JAKE
               Don't worry about it. All is good.

                         SAMUEL
               But I insist. There must be
               something I can repay you with?

                         JAKE
               Nah, I'm glad things turned out okay.

                         SARAH
               Samuel, may I have a word with you?

                                                    (CONTINUED)

Samuel and Sarah quietly talk between themselves for a moment.

                    SAMUEL
               (to Jake)
          My sister and I were wondering if
          you would like to come to an Amish
          wedding tomorrow? Actually, it is
          my wedding. That is why we came to
          town, to pick up some supplies.

                    JAKE
          Congratulations! Is the whole Amish
          community gonna be there?

                    SAMUEL
          Yes of course! Normally, we do not
          invite the English, but I will let
          everyone know that you are my friend.

A subtle smile forms on Jake's face.

                    JAKE
          It would be an honor to go to your
          wedding, but is there any way someone
          could pick me up? These highly
          sophisticated pair of sticks are my
          only mode of transportation right now.

Sarah giggles slightly. Samuel looks at her.

                    SARAH
          What?

                    SAMUEL
               (to Jake)
          Yes, I am sure we can arrange
          something. Where are you staying?

                    JAKE
               (pointing)
          At the motel behind me. Room 7.

                    SAMUEL
          Is 9 in the morning good for you?

                    JAKE
          9 is awesome!

Confused, Samuel looks over at Sarah. She shrugs her shoulders.

                    SAMUEL
               (confused)
          Awesome?

                    JAKE
          It means I'm good with 9.

                    SAMUEL
          Ahhhhh, I understand! We shall see
          you tomorrow then.

                                                        (CONTINUED)

JAKE
Looking forward to it.

SAMUEL
Good day, Isaac.

Samuel and Sarah make their way to the buggy, while Jake makes his way back to the motel.

57 **INT. JACOBS' HOUSE/GRACIE'S BEDROOM - DAY**

Gracie helps Ella with trying on the wedding dress.

GRACIE
It is marvelous, Ella. I am certain
Samuel will like it.

ELLA
You believe so?

GRACIE
Without a doubt.

ELLA
Would you like to come to town with me?
I still have a few more furnishings to
select and I would need your assistance.

GRACIE
Yes, of course. It would be my pleasure.

ELLA
Wonderful!

As Ella continues arranging the dress on herself, a look of sadness form on Gracie's face. She gives a sigh of grief.

GRACIE
Do you truly want to marry him, Ella?

ELLA
What kind of question is that? Of
course I do!

GRACIE
Even though it was Father and
Mother who chose him for you?

ELLA
Father knows my heart and I will
love and respect Samuel like the
Lord commands me to.

GRACIE
But how can you love someone whom you
did not choose for yourself? Love can
not forced on anyone.

ELLA
You love them by faith.

(CONTINUED)

Gracie sighs with emotions and stares out the window.

                    GRACIE
          I want to confess something to you,
          but I am terrified to do so.

                    ELLA
          Terrified! Terrified of what?

                    GRACIE
          You might confess it to Father.

                    ELLA
          If you do not want me to confess it to
          Father, then I will not. Speak your mind.

Moment of silence as Gracie gathers her thoughts.

                    GRACIE
          Something is not right with me.
          Something I cannot explain.

                    ELLA
          Tell me.

                    GRACIE
          My belly burns with such deep
          emotions. Emotions that I have
          never felt before. I do not know
          what it is, or how to explain it.

                    ELLA
              (teasing)
          And by any chance, are these "emotions"
          you feel for any certain "brother" I know?

Gracie turns to Ella.

                    GRACIE
          No, he is not a brother.

                    ELLA
              (confused)
          Not a brother?
              (suspiciously)
          You are not referring to that man
          you and Abe rescued, are you?

                    GRACIE
          Yes. (sigh) Ever since I saw him, my
          mind will not settle. I do not know what
          it is, Ella. He is all I think about.

Gracie nods then sighs.

                    ELLA
              (with compassion)
          Oh, my beloved sister.

Ella gives Gracie a hug.

                                                    (CONTINUED)

                         GRACIE
                    (with happiness)
               I am burning inside with these
               magnificent, exceptionally
               wonderful feelings, and yet>>>
                    (with sadness)
               >>>these feelings deeply (sigh)...
               deeply bruise my heart.

Hug ends.

                         ELLA
               He is of the English. You know we
               do not mix with them. It is our
               way. It has always been our way.

                         GRACIE
               Yes... Yes, I am aware of that, but
               I cannot help feeling what I feel.
               (sigh) What should I do? Tell me what
               to do, Ella?

                         ELLA
               I wish I knew what to say, Gracie,
               but I do not, but let us inquire
               the Lord for his guidance. I have
               faith he will provide the answers
               you desperately seek.

SUPER WIDE:

Gracie and Ella kneel on the floor and hold hands.

58   **INT. MT. JOY MOTEL/ROOM 9 - DUSK**

Jake's on the bed reading Gracie's Bible.

DOOR: KNOCK-KNOCK!!!

59   **EXT. MT. JOY MOTEL/ROOM 9 - DUSK**

Jake (crutches in hands) opens the door, looks around, but doesn't
see anyone. He looks down and sees a bag with a note attached. He
pulls the note and reads it.

                         GRACIE(V.O.)
                    (note reads)
               Greetings Isaac. I hope and pray
               you are healing quickly. I have
               prepared a little meal for you. I
               pray you find it to your liking.
               Your friend in the Lord, Gracie.

A huge smile forms on Jake's face. He picks up the bag, places it
inside the room, and closes the door after him.

60   **EXT. SAMUEL'S FARM/OPEN FIELD - MORNING**

CHARITY and ARIEL, both in their lower 20's, along with Gracie, chit-chat with one another. Abe, and TIMMY, a sturdy looking brother in his 20's, approach them.

>   TIMMY
>   Good morning, Sisters.

All the girls greet him back. Ariel gives Abe a subtle smile, but Abe does not show any acknowledgment.

>   TIMMY
>   Any of you wonderful ladies want to
>   partner with me?

Timmy gazes directly at Gracie. Gracie looks the other away.

>   TIMMY
>   Charity?

>   CHARITY
>   Sure.

>   TIMMY
>   Great!

Abe and Timmy leave. Ariel sighs with emotion.

>   ARIEL
>   (to Gracie)
>   I know that I am not the loveliest
>   sister to ever walk the Earth, but
>   I deeply wished your brother would
>   show some interest in me.

>   GRACIE
>   My brother is shy. You know that.

>   ARIEL
>   Yes, but perhaps if you say
>   something to him.

>   GRACIE
>   What do you want me to say?

>   ARIEL
>   Tell him that I am interested.

>   GRACIE
>   If that is your wish, I will.

>   ARIEL
>   (with excitement)
>   You will, really!?

>   GRACIE
>   I will tell him, really.

>   ARIEL
>   You will not forget?

(CONTINUED)

                        GRACIE
            I will not forget. I promise.

                        ARIEL
            Thank you.

Ariel gives Gracie a hug and a kiss.

                        CHARITY
                    (with urgency)
            Gracie! Caleb's coming this way!

                        GRACIE
                    (rolling her eyes)
            Oh, just wonderful!

CALEB, a young man in his mid 20's comes on the scene. He
takes off his hat.

                        CALEB
            Hello Ariel, Charity.

                        ARIEL CHARITY
            Good morning, Caleb. Good morning, Caleb.

He turns to Gracie.

                        CALEB
            How is your day, Gracie?

                        GRACIE
            Good, yours?

                        CALEB
            Just splendid! Ella is very lovely
            in her wedding dress. What say you?

                        GRACIE
            How may I help you, Brother Caleb?

A nervous tone forms in Caleb's voice.

                        CALEB
            Would you... (swallows) Would you
            like to partner, you know, for the
            games and dances?

                        GRACIE
            I would, (clears throat) but I have
            not been feeling so well today.

                        CALEB
            Oh, I am sorry to hear that. What
            is the matter?

                        GRACIE
            I am not feeling well, that is all.

                                                    (CONTINUED)

                         CALEB
                 What is hurting you?

Gracie looks away, but doesn't answer him. An uncomfortable moment
befalls them. Charity and Ariel look at each other.

                         CALEB
                 Then perhaps another time.

                         GRACIE
                 Yes, another time.

Caleb puts on his hat.

                         CALEB
                     (greeting)
                 Ariel, Charity... Gracie.

Gracie gives him a fake smile as he passes by her.

                         CHARITY
                     (to Gracie)
                 He's been after you for months. Why do
                 you insist on refusing his friendship?

                         GRACIE
                 Because he desires more than
                 friendship, and you know that.

                         CHARITY
                 And what if he does? He is a fine man
                 and if you had any smarts, you would
                 ask your father to have him court you.

                         GRACIE
                 Caleb is not the answer to my prayers,
                 and besides, I do not like him.

                         CHARITY
                 Like him!? What is there to like? All you
                 need is a good man, and he is a good man.

                         GRACIE
                 I have a better idea, Charity. I say
                 you ask your father to have him court
                 you, since you find him so pleasing.
                 I believe that is a splendid idea.

                         CHARITY
                     (hesitantly)
                 Well... (clears throat) If he was as
                 fond of me as he is of you, I would.

                         GRACIE
                 Did I sense a slight hesitation in
                 your voice?

                         CHARITY
                 As I said, he does not care for me.

                                                        (CONTINUED)

                          ARIEL
          Oh my! Would you look at that!?

                          CHARITY
          What?

                          ARIEL
          That handsome brother over there!

                          CHARITY
          Where?

                          ARIEL
          In Samuel's carriage. Do you not see?

Gracie looks over.

GRACIE'S POV:

Samuel helps Jake get out of the buggy, then hands him the crutches.

                          CHARITY(O.S.)
          Oh my! He is a sight, no doubt.

Jake wears an overly sized Amish attire and an Amish hat.

GRACIE'S POSITION:

Gracie becomes overwhelmed with emotion.

61   **EXT. SAMUEL'S FARM/OPEN FIELD - DAY**

All the AMISH WEDDING GUESTS are seated. Men and boys on one side of
the isle, women and girls on the other.

ELLA & SAMUEL'S POSITION:

Ella and Samuel stand in the front of FATHER BISHOP, an older Amish
man in his 70's.

                          FATHER BISHOP
          Samuel and Ella, do you both confess
          and believe that God has ordained
          marriage to be a covenant between one
          husband and one wife, and do you also
          have the confidence that you are
          approaching marriage in accordance
          with our Biblical teachings?

          SAMUEL   ELLA
Yes.   Yes.

                          FATHER BISHOP
          Do you, Brother Samuel, have full
          faith that the Lord has given our
          sister, Ella, as a suitable marriage
          partner for you?

Samuel and Ella look into each other's eyes with delight.

                                                    (CONTINUED)

                         SAMUEL
          Most certainly, yes.

                         FATHER BISHOP
          Do you, Sister Ella, have full faith that
          the Lord has given our brother, Samuel,
          as a suitable marriage partner for you?

                         ELLA
          I do.

The guests give off a subtle laugh.

                         FATHER BISHOP
          You have to say "yes."

                         ELLA
                    (nervously)
          Yes.

JAKE'S POSITION:

Jake sits way in the back scanning the women's section but doesn't
see Gracie. The vows continue in the background.

                         FATHER BISHOP(O.S.)
          Do you, Samuel, promise your wife that
          if she should ever be in any bodily
          weakness, sickness, or any comparable
          circumstance, and in need of your
          helping hand, that you will care for
          her as is fitting for a godly husband?

                         SAMUEL(O.S.)
          Yes.

GRACIE'S POSITION:

Gracie scans the men's section until her eyes land>>>

                         FATHER BISHOP(O.S.)
          Likewise, Ella, do you promise your
          husband that if he should ever be in
          any bodily weakness, sickness, or any
          comparable circumstance, and in need
          of your helping hand, that you will care
          for him as is fitting for a godly wife?

>>>on CALEB.

                         ELLA(O.S.)
          Yes.

CALEB'S POSITION:

Caleb gives Gracie an acknowledging nod and smile.

                         FATHER BISHOP(O.S.)
          Do you both promise that you will
          never separate from one another,>>>

GRACIE'S POSITION:

Gracie responds to Caleb with a disingenuous smile.

>   FATHER BISHOP(O.S.)
>   >>>regardless of any difficult
>   circumstances that may arise, until
>   God will separate you by death?

ELLA & SAMUEL'S POSITION:

>   SAMUEL ELLA
>   Yes. Yes.

Father Bishop takes Ella's hand and Samuel's hand and place them on
top of each other.

>   FATHER BISHOP
>   May the God of Abraham, Isaac, and
>   Jacob be with you and help you live
>   together in accordance with our
>   Biblical teachings and traditions.
>   May he richly pour his blessings
>   upon you, and may all of your days
>   be spent together to honor God, each
>   other, and your family with your divine
>   love. This be done through our Lord
>   and Savior, Jesus Christ, Amen.

>   EVERYONE
>   Amen.

>   FATHER BISHOP
>   (to everyone)
>   As per our custom, the wedding
>   day is the only time we allow
>   public affection to be displayed.
>   (to Samuel)
>   Brother Samuel, you may kiss your bride.

Samuel gives Ella a quick hesitant kiss on the cheek.

>   FATHER BISHOP
>   Oh, you can do much better than
>   that. She is your wife now.

The congregation laughs. He gives her another quick nervous kiss on
the lips.

>   FATHER BISHOP
>   (to everyone)
>   They will have plenty of practice.
>   Believe me!

Everyone laughs.

62   **INT. SAMUEL'S FATHER'S BARN - DAY**

The barn is full of Amish fun. Music, dancing, games, etc...

JAKE'S POSITION:

Jake tries to get some food off the table, but has a hard time with his crutches. Charity and Ariel approach him.

                CHARITY
        Would you like us to help you?

                JAKE
        That would be great, thank you.
        Just put a little of everything.

Charity takes a plate and starts loading.

                CHARITY
        May we ask your name?

                JAKE
        Isaac. What's yours?

                CHARITY
        I am Charity, and this is my
        friend, Ariel.

                ARIEL
        Very nice to meet you.

                CHARITY
        Your accent is somewhat different than
        ours. What ordnung do you belong to?

                JAKE
          (confused)
        Ordnung?

Gracie comes over.

                GRACIE
        Hello, Isaac.

                JAKE
        Gracie! So we meet again.

                CHARITY
        Wait! You two know each other!?

                GRACIE
        Yes, yes we do.

                ARIEL
          (to Gracie)
        How?

                JAKE
        Gracie and her brother rescued>>>

Gracie gives him a subtle "no" with her head.

(CONTINUED)

                          JAKE
          >>>me from a car accident.

                          ARIEL
                (confused)
          Car accident?

                          CHARITY
          You mean you were in someone's car
          and they got into an accident?

                          JAKE
          It was my car.

Charity lays the plate of food on the table and they both leave
without saying a word.

                          JAKE
          What's the matter with them?

                          GRACIE
          We do not associate with outsiders,
          unless it is business.

                          JAKE
          So I've been told. But yet you're
          still here.

                          GRACIE
          Would you like to go for a walk, Isaac?
          It is hard to talk with all the noise.

CALEB'S POSITION:

Caleb witness Gracie and Jake leaving together. Pure jealousy burns
on his face.

63   **EXT. PRAIRIE FIELD/BEATEN PATH - DAY**

Gracie and Jake(with crutches) walk on a beaten path in the middle
of the prairie field.

                          JAKE
          ...and that's how I came to the wedding.
          He even lent me a suit. What you think?

                          GRACIE
          It is slightly big on you, is it not?

                          JAKE
          It's all he had, but at least the
          hat fits nicely.

Gracie gives off a subtle laugh.

                          JAKE
          What's so funny?

                         GRACIE
              You have it on backwards.

                         JAKE
              I do?

Gracie takes it and puts it on the right way.

                         GRACIE
              There. You are one of us now.

                         JAKE
              Yeah, I guess I am.

They both laugh lightly.

                         JAKE
              Are there other Amish places like
              yours anywhere else?

                         GRACIE
              Yes. We have Amish communities
              scattered all over the country.

                         JAKE
              Oh wow! Did you ever visit any of them?

                         GRACIE
              I personally have not, but others
              do quite often.

                         JAKE
              Don't tell me they take the buggy!

Gracie laughs a bit.

                         GRACIE
              No. We mostly use the bus, but we
              also use the train and taxi.

                         JAKE
              Ahhhhhhh.

Moment of silence arises between them.

                         GRACIE
              Are you a believer, Isaac?

                         JAKE
              A believer?

                         GRACIE
              You know, do you believe in God
              and Jesus?

                         JAKE
              If I did, I don't remember.

                         GRACIE
              Yes, I understand.

Moment of silence as they continue walking.

                                                (CONTINUED)

                              JAKE
          Thank you for lending me your Bible,
          though. I've read John, Acts, and
          I've just started Romans.

                              GRACIE
          You have?

                              JAKE
          Yes I have.

                              GRACIE
          That is great! Let me know if you
          need help understanding anything.

                              JAKE
          I will.

They continue walking.

                              GRACIE
          You must think of us as crazy, you
          know, for living this simplistic
          lifestyle?

                              JAKE
          No, I don't think that. I don't
          think that at all.

                              GRACIE
          You can be honest with me, Isaac. I
          am not going to hate you for it. I
          sometimes wonder, too.

Jake crutches a step in front of her. They stop walking.

                              JAKE
          Well, I am curious to know why you choose
          to live this way. To me, technology
          makes people's lives easier, so why
          not embrace it? Why reject something
          that can make your life better?

                              GRACIE
          We do not reject all technology, Isaac,
          only the technology that has the power
          to separate us into individuals.

                              JAKE
          So what's wrong with a little
          individualism? I see it as freedom
          of self-expression.

                              GRACIE
          Nothing wrong with it. America was
          founded on rugged individualism, but our
          community was not. The foundation of our
          faith is in God, and each other. We need
          God and each other to survive, otherwise
          we become like everyone else in the world,
          and that is not who we are as a people.

                                                  (CONTINUED)

Moment of silence as Jake takes it in.

                    JAKE
          And what about phones? How come you
          don't use them?

                    GRACIE
          Well, we do use public phones, but only
          for emergencies and special occasions.
          We do not have them in our homes because
          they have a great potential to separate
          us from each other. You might believe it
          is nonsense, but let us suppose you and
          I needed to talk to someone. We get into
          our buggy, drive to their homes, and we
          sit and talk. They serve us with a little
          meal and we form a direct relationship
          with the whole family. It is more work,
          true, but if we replace that with a phone,
          we lose that person to person bond, that
          person to person touch. Oh my! Would you
          listen to me ramble!

                    JAKE
          You're not rambling, Gracie. I do
          want to understand your ways.

                    GRACIE
          You do?

                    JAKE
          Yes, I do. And you know what? Now I
          understand why you don't use phones.

                    GRACIE
          Really?

                    JAKE
          Uh-huh, and I've got the perfect
          example. Let's just say I'd rather
          be right here talking with you in
          person, than anywhere else in the
          world talking with you on the phone.

Gracie blushes with a smile, then nods.

                    GRACIE
          Yes, you have it.

64   **EXT. SAMUEL'S FARM/OPEN FIELD - DAY**

Jake and Gracie arrive from their walk. Caleb comes to them.

                    CALEB
          You are feeling much better, I see.

                    GRACIE
          Yes, much better.

                                              (CONTINUED)

                         CALEB
          Your father is searching for you.
          Where have you been this whole time?

                         GRACIE
          Why? Is something the matter?

                         CALEB
          He is concerned where you went.

                         GRACIE
          I was with Isaac.

                         CALEB
          That is what he is concerned about.

                         GRACIE
          I see.
                    (to Jake)
          Thank you for the wonderful
          conversation, Isaac. Be blessed.

Gracie leaves.

                         CALEB
          So you are that English man
          everyone is ranting about? What
          brings you here, and why are you
          wearing our sacred clothes?

                         JAKE
          I came here invited.

                         CALEB
          Invited by whom?

                         JAKE
          By the groom.

                         CALEB
          So you pretend to know the groom.
          What is his name?

                         JAKE
          Samuel, and his last name is Yoder,
          if you need to know.

                         CALEB
          I still do not believe you.

                         JAKE
          And who are you, exactly, that I
          need to justify myself to?

                         SAMUEL(O.S.)
          There you are, Isaac!

Samuel approaches them.

(CONTINUED)

                         SAMUEL
         I have been looking all over for
         you. I hope I am not interrupting
         anything of great importance?

                         JAKE
         Nothing at all. In fact we just finished.
              (to Caleb)
         Isn't that right?

                         CALEB
         Indeed.

                         SAMUEL
         Oh good! The elders have something
         very important to talk to you about.

                         JAKE
              (surprised)
         Talk to me!? About what!?

                         SAMUEL
         You will see soon enough.
              (greeting)
         Brother Caleb.

Samuel and Jake leave as they chit-chat. Pure envy forms on
Caleb's face.

65   **INT. SAMUEL'S FATHER'S BARN/ANOTHER ROOM - DAY**

Samuel and Jake(with crutches) stand in front of SEVEN AMISH
ELDERS, one of them being CHIEF ELDER. All of them older looking
men, 60 and up.

                         SAMUEL
         ...and perhaps Isaac could teach us
         some of his protective skills so we
         could protect our loved ones in time
         of need.

                         AMISH ELDER #1
         These "skills" you speak of sound
         like fighting, Brother Samuel, and
         you know well we do not tolerate
         such behavior.

                         SAMUEL
         It is not fighting, my brother. It
         is protecting.

                         AMISH ELDER #2
         I agree with my fellow brother. I
         do not see the difference between
         fighting and protecting.

                         SAMUEL
         When a pack of wolves attack our sheep,
         do we run, or do we stand up and protect
              (MORE)

                          SAMUEL(cont'd)
          our sheep? Of course we protect
          our sheep; each one of us does. Why
          then is it right to stand up for
          our sheep, but not right to stand
          up for the ones we love? Today God
          blessed my life with a wonderful wife.
          I need to know that I can protect her
          in time of need. Not only her, but my
          own children, and I am certain some
          of you share that same sentiment.

                          AMISH ELDER #3
                    (to Amish Elders)
          The Brother makes a valid point!

                          AMISH ELDER #4
          Indeed he does!

The elders talk among themselves.

                          CHIEF ELDER
          Let us vote.
                    (to Elders)
          How many of you favor your sons to
          familiarize themselves with these
          "protective skills" Samuel speaks of?

Three elders raise their hand in favor.

                          CHIEF ELDER
                    (to Samuel)
          The elders have voted and we have
          an equal amount on both sides.

                          SAMUEL
          Yes, but you could request to break
          the tie. It has been done before.

                          CHIEF ELDER
          We only follow this procedure
          under special circumstances.

                          SAMUEL
          And you do not believe this is
          a special circumstance?

Chief Elder ponders for a moment.

                          CHIEF ELDER
          Any possibility these teachings
          can be used on wolf attacks?

Samuel turns to Jake. Jake ponders for a tad.

                          JAKE
          I could improvise the teachings
          to be used for that purpose.

The 6 Elders chat among themselves, some favorably, some not.

                                              (CONTINUED)

                        CHIEF ELDER
                     (to 6 Elders)
               How many among you grant me
               permission to break the tie?

Four raise their hands.

                        CHIEF ELDER
               Brother Samuel, will you take it
               upon yourself to care for all of
               Isaac's needs?

                        SAMUEL
               All his needs will be met. This I
               promise before God and before this
               congregation.

                        CHIEF ELDER
               What say you, Isaac? Will you
               teach our sons these protective
               skills of yours?

                        JAKE
               It would be an honor.

                        CHIEF ELDER
               Very well, Brother Samuel. I grant
               you this request, but I also ask of
               you one other thing. That you teach,
               Isaac to respect our laws, our ways,
               and our traditions.
                     (to Jake)
               Isaac, would you be willing
               to learn our ways?

                        JAKE
               If Samuel teaches me your ways, I
               will respect them.

                        SAMUEL
                     (to Chief Elder)
               It shall be done.

                        JAKE
               But I also have a condition of my
               own, if you don't mind.

                        CHIEF ELDER
               What is your condition?

                        JAKE
               I don't want to be treated as an
               outsider during my stay. I want to
               be treated as one of you, like any
               other brother in the community.

                        CHIEF ELDER
               And why do you request this, Isaac?

                         JAKE
          Well, because if I am required to learn
          your ways, then I also need to practice
          your ways. How can I practice your ways,
          if I'm treated as an outsider?

                         CHIEF ELDER
          Fair enough. Meeting adjourned.

                         SAMUEL
                    (to Jake)
          This is such wonderful news, Isaac!
          Come! Let us pass it to the others.

VOCAL FAITH SONG BEGINS...

66   **ONE MONTH MONTAGE**

       Jake starts training with a handful of students in an open field,
       but with time, more and more boys show up.

       Samuel teaches Jake the laws and traditions of the Amish.

       Jake works alongside Samuel, learning all sorts of Amish farming
       methods and techniques.

       While at church, Gracie and Jake continue eyeing and chatting with
       one another. Caleb burns with deep jealousy.

       At the end of the montage, the class has about 20 Amish boys,
       learning Jake's skills and learning how to defend themselves from
       wolf attacks using a shepherd's staff.

       This montage is intercut with a sub-montage of Jake visiting Sheriff
       Phil, but still no luck finding the car.

67   **INT. AMISH CHURCH - DAY**

       We see a full congregation. Women on one side, men on the other. A
       sermon is in session. Jake peers over at Gracie. Gracie takes notice
       and gives him a beautiful bright smile.

       AMISH ELDER'S POSITION:

       Amish Elder #1 and Amish Elder #2 take notice of it, nodding at one
       another with deep concern.

       CALEB'S POSITION:

       Caleb sees the unfavorable reaction of the Elders. A creepy smile
       forms on his face.

       VOCAL FAITH SONG ENDS.

68   INT. AMISH CHURCH - DAY (LATER)

MR. JACOBS' POSITION:

Mr. Jacobs finishes chatting with a brother. Amish Elder #1
and Amish Elder #2 approach him.

                    AMISH ELDER #1
          Hope everything is well, Brother Jacobs?

                    MR. JACOBS
          Better than I deserve. Praise the Lord!

                    AMISH ELDER #2
          We have some deep concerns we would
          like to share with you, if you have
          a moment to discuss it.

                    MR. JACOBS
          What concerns do you have, my brothers?

Amish Elder #2 looks over at #1.

                    AMISH ELDER #1
          It has been brought to our attention
          that your daughter Gracie has taken
          a liking toward that English man.

GRACIE'S POSITION:

Gracie notices the two Elders talking to her father.

MR. JACOBS' POSITION:

                    AMISH ELDER #1
          We are deeply concerned where this
          infatuation may lead.

                    MR. JACOBS
                (inquiring)
          Lead?

                    AMISH ELDER #1
          As you are aware, my brother, we do
          not mingle with the English. That
          has always been our way.

                    MR. JACOBS
          I was under the impression that we
          were to treat Isaac as fellow brother.

The Amish Elders look at one another.

                    AMISH ELDER #1
          Yes-yes, that was the agreement, but
          in our humble estimation, it would be
          wise to keep Gracie at a distance, or
          otherwise she may become conformed by
          his worldly teachings and ideas. As it
          is said, "Bad associations corrupts
          good manners."

                                        (CONTINUED)

Mr. Jacobs ponders for a tad.

                    MR. JACOBS
          Thank you for sharing your concerns
          with me, brothers. I will look into
          the matter myself. Good day.

Amish Elder #1 and #2 look at each other.

                    AMISH EDLER #1
          Good day, Brother Jacobs.

                    AMISH ELDER #2
          Good day.

They leave.

69   **EXT. AMISH COUNTRY/CHURCH PREMISES - DAY**

Gracie is seated in the back of the buggy. Mr. Jacobs takes a seat
in the driver's seat and picks up the driving straps.

                    GRACIE
          What did the Elders want, Father?

                    MR. JACOBS
          They inquired about my health.

                    GRACIE
          They seemed terribly concerned about--

                    MR. JACOBS
          Nothing that concerns you, my daughter.

                    GRACIE
          Yes, Father.

Caleb enters.

                    CALEB
          Greetings, Brother Jacobs. What a
          splendid day, yes?

                    MR. JACOBS
          Yes, Praise God.

                    CALEB
          Praise God, indeed. Would it be
          well if I had a short discourse
          with your daughter?

                    MR. JACOBS
          You may, Brother Caleb.

Caleb turns to Gracie.

                    CALEB
          Hello, Gracie. Splendid day, yes?

                              GRACIE
                         (rolling her eyes)
                    What do you want, Caleb?

                              MR. JACOBS
                    That is not the proper way to
                    talk to a brother, Gracie.

                              GRACIE
                         (with humbleness)
                    Yes, Father.

Mrs. Jacobs enters.

                              MRS. JACOBS
                    May I help you with something,
                    Brother Caleb?

                              CALEB
                    I am having a chat with your
                    charming daughter.

                              MRS. JACOBS
                    You are much too kind. You may
                    continue your chat another day.

                              CALEB
                    Very well. Good day, Gracie.

                              MR. JACOBS
                    Would you like to have dinner
                    with us, Brother Caleb?

                              MRS. JACOBS GRACIE
                    No!!! No!!!

                              MR. JACOBS
                    No?

                              MRS. JACOBS
                         (to Mr. Jacobs)
                    I already invited Ella and Samuel
                    for dinner.
                         (to Caleb)
                    I am terribly sorry, Brother Caleb.
                    Perhaps another time.

                              MR. JACOBS
                    But I am sure we can add one
                    additional plate to the table, can
                    we not?
                         (to Caleb)
                    What do you say, Brother Caleb?

Caleb looks over at Gracie's unhappy face.

                                                        (CONTINUED)

70   **INT. JACOBS' HOUSE/DINING ROOM - DAY**

Jake, Mr. Jacobs, Samuel, Abe, and Caleb, are all gathered around
the dinner table.

                    CALEB
              (with self-admiration)
          And I pulled that stubborn goat out of
          that deep ditch with my bare hands. It
          is hard to imagine, I understand, but
          it is the God honest truth.

Caleb humors himself with laughter.

                    JAKE
          You must pump iron.

                    CALEB
              (confused)
          Pump iron? I do not understand.

                    JAKE
          You know?

Jake goes up and down with his arms as if he's lifting dumbbells.
Caleb's still confused.

                    JAKE
          Never mind.

                    MR. JACOBS
          How is the farm coming, Samuel? Are
          you done with planting?

                    SAMUEL
          Yes, Father. With Isaac's help, I
          finished a week ago.

                    MR. JACOBS
          Oh really!? What did he help you with?

                    SAMUEL
          Ask him, Father. He will tell you.

Moment of silence.

                    MR. JACOBS
          How are the teachings coming
          along, Isaac? My ears have heard
          some great things.

                    JAKE
          It's going well, Sir. Everyone in
          the class has made much progress.
              (to Caleb)
          How come you're not taking my
          class, Caleb?

                    CALEB
          I hold the belief that fighting is
          from the Devil.

                                            (CONTINUED)

                    SAMUEL
                (defensive)
        It is not fighting, Brother Caleb. It
        is protecting. There is a difference.

                    CALEB
        I will not be swayed in any
        direction. We will have to agree
        to disagree, Brother Samuel.

                    SAMUEL
        Indeed we will.

                    MR. JACOBS
                (to Jake)
        It would be great if Abe would
        familiarize himself with your
        teachings, but there is so little
        time. Ever since the accident, I
        have not been much of a man. Abe
        works hard enough for both of us.

                    SAMUEL
        Do you need help, Father? I could
        spare a day or two.

                    MR. JACOBS
        I appreciate the offer, Samuel, but
        I cannot accept.

                    SAMUEL
        But why, Father?

                    MR. JACOBS
        You and Ella have only begun your
        lives together. It is too much to
        ask, my son.

                    JAKE
        I could help you, Sir.

                    CALEB
        You!? What could you possibly do?

                    JAKE
                (to Mr. Jacobs)
        Everything Samuel has taught me, I
        can do, Mr. Jacobs.

                    CALEB
        And I certainly know why.

                    MR. JACOBS
                (to Caleb)
        Would you be willing to lend my son
        a helping hand, Brother Caleb? It
        would only be 2 days a week.

Caleb clears his throat.

(CONTINUED)

                         CALEB
               I am truly honored by your offer,
               Brother Jacobs, but I respectfully
               have to decline. My father has still
               not finished planting.

                         SAMUEL
               I chatted with your father at
               church. He says planting is done.

Caleb clears his throat once again.

                         CALEB
               He must have finished it without
               my knowledge.

                         MR. JACOBS
                    (to Caleb)
               I would pay you rightly, Brother Caleb.

                         CALEB
               Many regrets, but I cannot. I am much
               too busy with personal things.

Caleb clears his throat once again and swallows with guilt.
Mr. Jacobs realizes Caleb is talking smack.

                         MR. JACOBS
               I see.
                    (to Jake)
               Tell me, Isaac, why do you feel
               compelled to offer yourself?

                         JAKE
               Well, Sir,... Abe and Gracie saved my life.
               It would not be right if I didn't repay
               them in some way. This would be my chance.

                         MR. JACOBS
               And what do you want in return?

                         JAKE
               Food and a room is all I need.

                         MR. JACOBS
               We could convert one of the horse
               stalls into a guest room. Would
               that be suitable to you?

                         JAKE
               Yes, that would be fine.

Moment of silence as Mr. Jacobs ponders on the idea.

                         MR. JACOBS
               Very well, Isaac. I will discuss it
               with Mrs. Jacobs and inform you of
               our decision tomorrow.

Jealousy burns on Caleb's face.

                         CALEB
          You are not seriously contemplating
          of allowing this wretched English man,
          who is clearly infatuated with your
          daughter, to dwell here?

                         MR. JACOBS
                    (calm)
          Brother Caleb, it would not be wise
          of me to remind you whose home your
          feet are planted. Would it?

An expression of shock followed by deep discontent, forms on Caleb's
face. Mrs. Jacobs, Ella, and Gracie bring out the dishes and set them
on the table, then take their seats.

                         MRS. JACOBS
          Ella baked us baby lamb chops.

                         MR. JACOBS
          Thank you, Ella. Much appreciated.

                         MRS. JACOBS
          Mr. Jacobs! These are not just lamb
          chops, these are "baby" lamb chops.

                         MR. JACOBS
          Yes, I understand.
                    (to Ella)
          May the Lord bless you immensely,
          Ella for your baby lamb chops.

Ella holds her belly with one hand, takes Samuel's hand, and stares
into his eyes with delight.

                         ELLA
          He already has.

                         SAMUEL
          Indeed, he has.

Gracie and Jake eye one another and smile.

                         MR. JACOBS
                    (confused)
          What are you saying, my daughter?
          Are you expecting?

Moment of silence.

                         ELLA
          YES!!!

They celebrate the news with hugs and kisses. Jake and Caleb do not
join in the celebration.

                         MR. JACOBS
          Brother Caleb, would you honor us
          with the blessing for this meal?

                        CALEB
          Thank you, Brother Jacobs, but I would
          like to pass the honor to Brother Isaac.
                (to Jake)
          What do you say, "Brother Isaac?" Will you
          honor us with a prayer from the heart?

Jake is caught by surprise.

                        JAKE
          Yeah... sure.

Everyone bows. A long uncomfortable silence forms between them for
Jake doesn't know what to say.

                        MR. JACOBS
          I will say the blessing.

                        JAKE
          No-no. I can do it.

Jake ponders for a moment.

                        JAKE
                (Matthew 6:9-13(KJV))
          "(9)...Our Father which art in heaven,
          Hallowed be thy name. (10) Thy kingdom
          come, Thy will be done in earth, as it is
          in heaven. (11) Give us this day our daily
          bread. (12) And forgive us our debts, as
          we forgive our debtors. (13) And lead us not
          into temptation, but deliver us from evil:
          For thine is the kingdom, and the power,
          and the glory, for ever. Amen."

                        EVERYONE
          Amen!

                        CALEB
                (mockingly)
          Ahhhhh, the Lord's prayer. How convenient.

                        SAMUEL
          It is the Lord's word, Brother
          Caleb. Is it not?

                        CALEB
          Indeed, but we were expecting a
          prayer from within. Were we not?

                        SAMUEL
          We expected nothing. The prayer was
          good. Let it be.

                        JAKE
                (to everyone)
          How should I have prayed?

> CALEB
> (prideful)
> It would be an honor to show you,
> that is if
> (to Mr. Jacobs)
> it sits well with Brother Jacobs.

> MR. JACOBS
> (to Caleb)
> You may save your prayer for another
> time, Brother Caleb.
> (to everyone)
> Let us enjoy this wonderful meal while
> it is still hot.

> CALEB
> Yes, everyone. Let us eat and be merry,
> for today we live and tomorrow we die.

An awkward moment fills the air. They begin to chit-chat between themselves, but nobody chats with Caleb.

> CALEB
> (to everyone)
> Excuse me, brothers and sisters. It has
> come to mind that my presence is needed
> somewhere else. My apologies for such
> an abrupt exit. Good day!

Caleb gets up and leaves. Everyone is stunned.

71   **EXT. JACOBS' FARM/FRONT PORCH - DAY**

Jake sits on the front porch bench. BROTHER ABRAMS, an Amish man in his 60's, passes by Mr. Jacobs house in a buggy.

> JAKE
> Good day, Brother Abrams.

Jake lifts his arm in the air.

> BROTHER ABRAMS
> Good day, Brother Isaac. What a
> delightful day.

> JAKE
> Yes it is.

Gracie comes out of the house.

> GRACIE
> So this is where you are hiding?

> JAKE
> It's quiet here.

Gracie sits across from him.

> GRACIE
> I like the quiet too.

(CONTINUED)

Moment of silence arises between them.

> GRACIE
> How did you know the Lord's prayer by heart?

> JAKE
> I don't know. It just came to me.

> GRACIE
> Your memory is slowly coming back.
> That is good.

> . JAKE
> Yeah, it is.

Moment of silence.

> GRACIE
> No luck finding the car?

> JAKE
> No... But I'm not in any hurry.

> GRACIE
> What if they never find it? What
> will you do then?

> JAKE
> I don't know... Maybe I'll find a
> nice Amish wife and settle down
> with a few kids.

> GRACIE
> (teasing)
> Ohhhhh, so that is your plan? Are
> you by any chance eyeing anyone?

> JAKE
> As of matter of fact, I am.

> GRACIE
> Oh really! Anyone in particular?

> JAKE
> I'm afraid if I say her name, Caleb
> might try to steal her from me.

They both laugh. After a moment, they look into each other's eyes
and smile with delight.

72   **INT. JACOBS' FARM/HOME/JACOBS' BEDROOM - NIGHT**

Mrs. Jacobs reads the Bible in bed with her head covering off. Long
graceful hair flows down to her waist. Mr. Jacobs walks in the
bedroom and slips underneath the sheets.

> MR. JACOBS
> Every day you become more and more lovely,
> Mrs. Jacobs. How is that even possible?

(CONTINUED)

He tries to kiss her on the cheek, but she turns away.

                    MR. JACOBS
          Okay, what did I do?

                    MRS. JACOBS
          Did you have to invite Caleb?

                    MR. JACOBS
          I did it for Gracie.

                    MRS. JACOBS
               (surprised)
          For Gracie!?

                    MR. JACOBS
          She needed a teaching to be proper with every
          brother, not just brothers she cares for.

She ponders on his comment for a moment.

                    MRS. JACOBS
          Yes, she is slightly rude with
          brothers she does not care for.

                    MR. JACOBS
          And I wonder where she gets it from?

                    MRS. JACOBS
          Oh stop!

He laughs lightly.

                    MRS. JACOBS
          We witnessed a side of Caleb we did

               not see before. Did we not?

                    MR. JACOBS
          Indeed. Not the kind of son I would
          care to have in our family.

                    MRS. JACOBS
          Nor I, for that matter.

She closes the Bible and sets it on the nightstand.

                    MR. JACOBS
          Isaac offered to help us with planting.

                    MRS. JACOBS
               (surprised)
          He did!?

                    MR. JACOBS
          Yes. What do you say? Should we accept?

                    MRS. JACOBS
          I admire Isaac. He seems like a very
          good and proper English boy.

(CONTINUED)

                    MR. JACOBS
            He may be proper, but he does see
            our daughter, and that concerns me.

                  MRS. JACOBS
            Yes... Timmy, Caleb, and all the other
            brothers alike. Gracie is a sight to
            behold, is she not?

                  MR. JACOBS
            Yes, it is true, but the others are just
            that, brothers. Isaac is of the English.

                  MRS. JACOBS
            We cannot allow Abe to continue working
            the farm by himself. If Isaac is willing,
            I say yes. Samuel and Ella are very fond
            of him, and so am I.

                  MR. JACOBS
            And what makes you to be so "fond" of him?

                  MRS. JACOBS
            I do not believe I have to say it,
            Mr. Jacobs. You already know.

Mrs. Jacobs looks at him with a twinkle in her eye.

                  MR. JACOBS
            Oh no! Not even a hint of closeness.

                  MRS. JACOBS
            And I beg to differ.

                  MR. JACOBS
            Beg all you wish. Not even close.

Moment of silence as the conversation settles.

                  MR. JACOBS
            It would be beneficial for Abe to take
            those protective teachings. We have
            not had a wolf attack in a while, thank
            the Lord for that, but if and when we
            have another, he should be prepared.

                  MRS. JACOBS
            This, I agree.

After a moment, he gives her a kiss on the cheek.

                  MR. JACOBS
            Very well. I will take it to the Lord and see
            what he has to say. Goodnight, Mrs. Jacobs.

                  MRS. JACOBS
            Good night, Mr. Jacobs, or should I say--

                  MR. JACOBS
            Don't be bad, Leah.

She laughs.

73   **EXT. RITZY HIGH-RISE/FRONT GATE - DAY**

MYSTERIOUS MAN, dressed in a high-class business suit, walks up to
the front gate of Jake's ritzy high-rise. Only his back is visible.
He presses the "PRESS HERE FOR HELP," button. A female voice, with
a Swedish accent, comes over a speaker.

> SWEDISH GIRL(V.O.)
> Welcome to Bella Towers. How may I
> help you?

> MYSTERIOUS MAN
> I'm here to visit an old friend.
> Jake Daniels.

> SWEDISH GIRL(V.O.)
> Oh, I am terribly sorry. Jake
> hasn't come back from his trip.

> MYSTERIOUS MAN
> Well, I have something of his.
> Would you give it to him when
> he gets back? It's small.

> SWEDISH GIRL(V.O.)
> Sure, absolutely! Just place it
> inside the box on your right.

A little door opens. A shiny gold pen with initials "JTID," drops in
the box with a folded note in the clip.

74   **EXT. AMISH COUNTRY ROAD/CARRIAGE - DAY (TRAVELING)**

Jake and Abe ride in the carriage as they chat.

> ABE
> ...That is why all the women wear the head
> covering. Husbands are the only ones
> permitted to see their wives uncovered.

> JAKE
> What about other women?

> ABE
> Other woman is permitted. Only the
> man is not.

> JAKE
> I understand.

Moment of silence as the buggy strolls along.

> ABE
> I appreciate you doing this, Brother
> Isaac. I cannot thank you enough.

> JAKE
> You're welcome, Abe. Is it okay if
> I call you, Abe?

(CONTINUED)

                         ABE
          Yes, that is good. I need to confess
          something to you, Brother Isaac.
          It has been shaming me for weeks.

                         JAKE
          Please, call me Isaac. What do you
          want to confess?

Abe hesitates for a moment.

                         ABE
          That day we saved you. (sigh) It was not
          I who saved you. We both saw what happened,
          but I did not want to get involved. If it
          were not for Gracie (swallows)... we
          would not be chatting at this moment...
          I beg your forgiveness for my sinful act.

                         JAKE
          Don't worry about it, Abe. All is good...
          I'd like to confess something too, but...
          Would you keep it between us?

                         ABE
          I will not confess it to anyone,
          if that is your desire.

Jake ponders for a tad.

                         JAKE
          I like your sister, Abe. She is such
          a wonderful person to be around.

                         ABE
          Yes, I know, Isaac. The liking for my
          sister is visible. Everyone sees it.

                         JAKE
                     (embarrassed)
          Oh!

Moment of silence.

                         JAKE
          Do you know how she feels about me?

                         ABE
          That I do not know. It is not permissible
          for a woman to share her feelings with
          another man, unless it is her husband,
          or she is courting.

The carriage rolls out of the shot.

75   **EXT. JACOBS' FARM - DAY**

Abe pulls the carriage in front of the barn. Bark barks for
attention. Jake approaches the dog.

                                              (CONTINUED)

                         JAKE
                      (to Bark)
                 Hey, boy! How you doing?

He pets him and scratches his ears.

                         JAKE
                      (to Abe)
                 What's his name?

                         ABE
                 Bark.

                         JAKE
                 Bark!? Really!?

                         ABE
                 We named him that because he
                 likes barking at everything.

                         JAKE
                 Ahhhhh...

He plays with the dog for a moment.

                         JAKE
                    Sit, boy.

The dog sits.

                         JAKE
                 Roll over.

He rolls over.

                         JAKE
                 You taught him well.

                         ABE
                 Not sure where he learnt that.
                 Come, I will show you to your room.

76   **INT. JACOBS' BARN/JAKE'S ROOM - DAY**

The door opens. Abe and Jake enter. We see a bed in the corner, with
a table and two chairs beside it.

                         ABE
                 It is not much, I know.

                         JAKE
                 No, it's fine. When do I start?

                         ABE
                 Tomorrow morning. We wake up at 4.

                         JAKE
                 Okay. I'll be ready.

77   **INT. JACOBS' BARN/JAKE'S ROOM - NIGHT**

Jake finishes arranging his room. He makes his way to the bed, blows
out the candle, and tries to sleep. Suddenly, he hears barking,
scratching, and whining.

                    JAKE
          What the?

Again; barking, scratching, and whining.

78   **EXT. JACOBS' BARN - NIGHT**

Jake exits the barn with a candle in his hand.

                    JAKE
               (to Bark)
          Hey! What's with all the noise?

Bark whines a tad.

                    JAKE
          What?

He whines some more.

                    JAKE
          I don't understand.

Bark gets down on all fours, as if he's begging.

                    JAKE
          Oh, you must be lonely out here all
          by yourself... You're welcome to
          sleep in my room, if you like.

Bark gets up quickly and barks.

                    JAKE
          Promise me you're gonna tell me
          when you need to go.

Bark raises one paw in the air.

                    JAKE
          Okay, you got yourself a deal.

Jake shakes his paw.

VOCAL FAITH SONG BEGINS...

79   **THREE WEEK MONTAGE**

We see a three-week montage of Jake working on Jacobs' farm; tilling
the soil, planting, fixing up the place. Taking care of the animals.
          (cows, goats, sheep, horses, etc...)

Abe teaches Jake how to ride a horse.

                                                      (CONTINUED)

This montage is intercut with Jake teaching his protective skills on Mr. Jacobs' farm.

Jake chops wood by the barn. Gracie walks out of the barn with a pail of milk and gives him a bright smile. He bows his hat to her and smiles back. She passes by Mr. Jacobs and immediately she wipes the smile off her face.

Bark and Jake form a strong bond. Bark is always with him.

Jake continues to check on his car, but still no luck.

VOCAL FAITH SONG ENDS.

80   **EXT. JACOBS' FARM/FIELD - DAY**

Abe, with a shepherd's staff in his hand, tends the sheep.

WOLVES' POSITION:

A pack of wolves quietly sneaks out of the woods.

81   **EXT. JACOBS' FARM/FENCE - DAY**

Jake fixes a portion of the fence. Bark yawns beside him.

                    JAKE
          It's finished! Thank you, God!
               (to Bark)
          Not bad, huh?

Dog barks.

                    JAKE
          What do you think? Is there a God?
          Everyone here seems to believe so.

Bark gets up and licks his face.

                    JAKE
          Yuck! That's gross, Bark.

Jake wipes his face with his arm. Suddenly, Bark stares in a certain direction barks intensely.

                    JAKE
          What is it, boy?

Jake stands up and spots the wolves approaching the flock.

                    JAKE
          GO, BARK!

Bark takes off. Jake jumps on the horse.

                    JAKE
          HYAAAAAAAAA!!!

82   **EXT. JACOBS' FARM/FIELD - DAY**

The wolves strike. ABE uses his staff to fight them off.

83   **EXT. JACOBS' FARM/FIELD/FURTHER AWAY - DAY**

Bark runs with everything he has. Jake trails behind.

84   **EXT. JACOBS' FARM/FIELD - DAY**

Abe trips to the ground. The wolves quickly surround him. They are
about to strike when Bark tackles one of them. Jake fights off the
other wolves. In the end Jake is surrounded by 3 wolves, not really
knowing what to do.

                    ABE
          ISAAC!!!

Abe throws the shepherd's staff to Jake. Jake catches it and uses it
to attack the wolves. After some time, all the wolves scatter back
into the woods.

BARK'S POSITION:

Bark sadly whines as he circles a bloody tremoring sheep. Abe and
Jake approach the sheep as it slowly dies in their presence. Abe gets
down and holds the sheep's head.

                    ABE
          She was my favorite sheep.

                    JAKE
          Is there anything we can do?

                    ABE
          No. She will die.

The sheep dies. Tears flow down Abe's cheeks.

                    ABE
          There were just too many.

                    JAKE
          It's not your fault, Abe. It could
          have happened to anyone.

Abe notices the back of Jake's right hand bleeding.

                    ABE
          You are hurt, Isaac!

                    JAKE
          It's just a flesh wound. Nothing to
          worry about.

                    ABE
          May I have a look?

Jake shows Abe his hand.

(CONTINUED)

                              ABE
               It is deeper than a flesh wound, Isaac.

Jake pulls back his hand.

                              JAKE
               I'm fine. What do we do with the sheep?

                              ABE
               We do not eat animals defiled
               by other animals.

                              JAKE
               So we bury her?

                              ABE
               It is our way, yes.

85   **EXT. JACOBS' FARM - BEFORE DUSK**

The sun is low on the horizon. With one hand bandaged, Jake teaches
the class under the shade of a huge tree. Timmy holds AMISH TEEN #1,
a tall-skinny brother in his 20's, so he can't move his arms.

                              JAKE
               What do you do when you can't use
               your arms?

Amish Teen #1 tries to break free, but can't.

                              AMISH TEEN #1
               I cannot breathe!

                              JAKE
               That's enough, Timmy.

Timmy lets go. Amish Teen #1 gasps for air.

                              TIMMY
               Are you well?

                              AMISH TEEN #1
               I will be once I catch my breath.

                              JAKE
               Now Timmy is going to hold me, but before
               he does, what do you think I will do?

ABE'S POSITION:

Amish Teen #1 takes a seat on the ground beside Abe, Samuel, and
AMISH TEEN #2, a short, plumpy looking fellow. Amish Teen #2 raises
his hand.

                              JAKE(O.S.)
Yes.

                    AMISH TEEN #2
          You will smash his brains in with your
          foot, then twist his head off till he dies.

Instant laughter breaks out.

                    AMISH TEEN #2
          What!? What I say!?

JAKE'S POSITION:

Jake laughs along with them.

                    JAKE
          No, not exactly!
               (to Timmy)
          You ready?

                    TIMMY
          Yes.

                    JAKE
          Hold me tight.

Timmy holds Jake tight. Jake pushes himself back, placing one leg
between Timmy's legs, tripping him. They both fall to the ground.
Timmy loosens his grip to catch his fall. As soon as they hit the
ground, Jake hits him across the chest with his good arm. Everyone
is awed by the maneuver.

AMISH TEEN #2 POSITION:

                    AMISH TEEN #2
          That is precisely what I would have
          done. Precisely!

                    AMISH TEEN #1
               (teasing)
          Oh suuuuuuuuure!

Everyone pokes fun at him.

                    AMISH TEEN #2
               (to everyone)
          No, really! I would have!

JAKE'S POSITION:

Jake helps Timmy get up.

                    JAKE
          You did well. Thanks for volunteering.
          That's it for today. See you next time.

As everyone leaves, Jake makes his way toward the tree trunk and sits
down, leaning with his back against it. BARK comes over and sniffs
his bandaged hand. Bark whines.

                    JAKE
          I'll be fine. Don't worry.

(CONTINUED)

Bark whines some more and sits down beside him.

> GRACIE(O.S.)
> That was really good, Isaac!

> JAKE
> (surprised)
> Gracie!

She takes a seat on the ground right in front of him.

> GRACIE
> I came to check your wound, if that
> is well with you.

> JAKE
> You may check away!

Moment of silence as Gracie takes off the bandage.

> JAKE
> You are as beautiful as an angel, Gracie.

She stops unfolding and blushes with delight.

> GRACIE
> You told me that before. It was the
> first thing you said to me when you
> opened your eyes. Remember?

> JAKE
> If my memory serves me correctly- no
> pun intended, I think the first thing
> I said was, "Am I in heaven?"

> GRACIE
> Yes. That is what you said, and I
> said, "No, but you came this close."

She shows him with her fingers.

> JAKE
> And then I said, "I have to be,
> because you are the prettiest angel
> I have ever seen in my life."

A bright smile forms on Gracie's face. After a moment, she unwinds
the last part of the bandage.

> GRACIE
> (with concern)
> Oh Isaac! Your hand looks horrible!

> JAKE
> It's fine, Gracie. It doesn't hurt a
> bit. OUCH! Okay, maybe it hurts a little.

> GRACIE
> How can you say that, Isaac? You
> need to see the doctor.

                                    JAKE
                    It just looks bad, but I'm fine.

                                    GRACIE
                              (with concern)
                    Please, Isaac. If you will not do it
                    for you, then do it for me. It would
                    make me so happy if you did. Please,
                    please see Dr. Collins. Please...

He places his good hand on her dazzling face.

                                    JAKE
                    There isn't anyone here who has
                    shown me more kindness and respect.

She sighs.

                                    JAKE
                    Okay. I'll do it for you.

86   **INT. JACOBS' HOUSE/KITCHEN - BEFORE DUSK**

Mrs. Jacobs slides the curtain to the side and peeks out the window.

MRS. JACOBS' POV:

Jake and Gracie are enjoying each other's company, as the golden-hour
sun shines beautifully on them.

                                    MR. JACOBS(O.S.)
                    What are you viewing, Mrs. Jacobs?

MRS. JACOBS' POSITION:

She quickly and guiltily lets go of the curtain.

                                    MRS. JACOBS
                    Oh, nothing! Nothing at all.

                                    MR. JACOBS
                    May I have a look?

Mr. Jacobs tries to take a peek, but Mrs. Jacobs blocks him.

                                    MRS. JACOBS
                    I asked Gracie to check Isaac's wound.

He moves over to have a look, but she moves with him.

                                    MR. JACOBS
                    Leah!

She hesitantly slides to the side. Mr. Jacobs pulls the curtain
and peeks through. He gives a sigh.

                                    MR. JACOBS
                    I was afraid of this, Mrs. Jacobs.

                         MRS. JACOBS
          Brings back memories, does it not?

                         MR. JACOBS
          It will never work.

                         MRS. JACOBS
          And why not? He is a good man and I
          respect him. Everyone respects him.

                         MR. JACOBS
          Do you believe he will stay and
          become one of us?

                         MRS. JACOBS
          Yes, I believe he would.

                         MR. JACOBS
          Oh, Leah, even if he does- Even if he
          does! He is of the English. The whole
          community will shun him, and they
          will shun us for even considering it.

                         MRS. JACOBS
          They are not shunning him now.

                         MR. JACOBS
          Only because they are using him, but
          deep down, they still treat him as an
          outsider. I know it and you know it.
          Do not be blinded by what you do not
          want to see. Things are the way they
          are and we need to accept that.

She walks over to the table and places her hands on top of one of
the chairs, then sighs with grief.

                         MRS. JACOBS
          I like him, Mr. Jacobs. He would
          treat her well. I know he would.

He walks over to comfort her, but she refuses.

                         MRS. JACOBS
                 (with rebuke)
          Why do you not see in him what I
          saw in you?

She leaves the room upset. He sighs with regret.

87   **INT. JACOBS' BARN/JAKE'S ROOM - NIGHT**

Jake reads the Bible at the table. He ponders for a moment.

                         JAKE
          Wow... That's deep.

He closes the Bible, blows out the candle, and hits the bed. Bark
jumps on the bed and lays at his feet.

                         JAKE
          Good night, Bark.

88   **INT. MT. JOY MEDICAL CLINIC - DAY**

Jake sits on the medical bed as Dr. Collins pulls the last stitch and
cuts the thread.

> DR. COLLINS
> There, all done! I'm glad you came
> before it got worse.

> JAKE
> How long do they stay in for?

> DR. COLLINS
> The stitches will fall out on their
> own. No need to come in. I'm also going
> to give you some medicine. Make sure
> you empty the whole bottle.

Dr. Collins hands Jake a prescription. Jake takes it.

> JAKE
> So that's it? I can go?

> DR. COLLINS
> One last thing to do.

Dr. Collins pulls out a syringe from his pocket with a long needle.
He takes off the needle cap and squirts some liquid.

> DR. COLLINS
> Which side?

Jake swallows hard with a genuine concern on his face.

> JAKE
> You sure that's necessary?

89   **EXT. MT. JOY MEDICAL CLINIC - DAY**

Abe stands by the horse/buggy. Caleb passes in a carriage.

> ABE
> Brother Caleb.

Caleb gives Abe a cold conniving stare as he passes, but doesn't
respond whatsoever. Jake enters rubbing his tush.

> JAKE
> Was that Caleb?

> ABE
> Yes, and he is up to no good.

> JAKE
> How do you know?

> ABE
> I just know.

90   **INT. MT. JOY LIBRARY - DAY**

Kloey sits behind the information desk talking on the phone.

>   KLOEY
>   Yup. It's all ready for you, Mrs.
>   Johnson. You can pick it up
>   anytime... Bye-bye.

She hangs up the phone and begins typing on the computer. Caleb enters the library and looks around in confusion. He pulls a book off the shelf half-way and pushes it back in. Kloey takes notice of him.

>   KLOEY
>   (surprised)
>   Oh! Good day, Sir!

>   CALEB
>   Good day, Ma'am.

>   KLOEY
>   What may I help you with?

>   CALEB
>   I am trying to trace my family
>   heritage and I was hoping you would
>   have a book for such a task.

>   KLOEY
>   Well, I'm not sure if we have such
>   a book for you, but you're more
>   than welcome to search the web.

>   CALEB
>   Where do I go to find this web place?

>   KLOEY
>   No, no. Come, I'll show you.

They leave.

91   **INT. JACOBS' HOUSE/KITCHEN - NIGHT**

Gracie puts the finishing touches on a plate of food.

>   GRACIE
>   (softly to herself)
>   It is perfect.

Mrs. Jacobs walks in.

>   MRS. JACOBS
>   Is that for Isaac?

>   GRACIE
>   Yes, Mother.

>   MRS. JACOBS
>   Let me get Abe-

(CONTINUED)

A charming smirk forms on Mrs. Jacobs' face.

                    MRS. JACOBS
          Abe is preoccupied with other
          things. I say you take it.

                    GRACIE
               (surprised)
          Me!?

                    MRS. JACOBS
          Yes. Do you not approve?

                    GRACIE
          What about Father?

                    MRS. JACOBS
          I will keep your father busy till
          you get back. What say you?

Gracie sighs deeply, but doesn't respond.

92   **INT. JACOBS' BARN/JAKE'S ROOM - NIGHT**

Jake pours himself a glass of water, then looks over the bottle of
pills. Bark sits on the bed.

                    JAKE
               (to himself)
          Take one in the morning and one in
          the evening, preferably after meals.

DOOR: KNOCK-KNOCK!

                    JAKE
          It's unlocked.

Gracie opens the door.

                    JAKE
               (surprised)
          Gracie! What a pleasant surprise.

Bark immediately goes to her. She pets him.

                    GRACIE
          How's my favorite dog?

Jake walks over to her.

                    GRACIE
          I brought you your food, Isaac.
          Where do you want me to set it?

Jake takes the plate from her.

                    JAKE
          Thank you. Did your father send you?

                                              (CONTINUED)

                         GRACIE
               No. Mother did.

                         JAKE
               Oh... Would you like to have a seat?

Gracie looks back, as if she's scared to hang around.

                         GRACIE
               I guess I can stay for a moment.

They make their way to the table and sit across from each
other. An awkward moment of silence arises between them.

                         JAKE
               The food looks great. Did you make it?

                         GRACIE
               I made the potatoes and the salad.

                         JAKE
               Do you mind if I try them right now?

                         GRACIE
               No, I do not mind.

Jake takes the fork and tries the potatoes.

                         JAKE
               Nobody makes potatoes like you,
               Gracie. Absolutely nobody!

Gracie chuckles.

                         GRACIE
               It's just potatoes, Isaac. We all
               make it the same.

                         JAKE
               Yes, but these potatoes were made
               with love, and that's the difference.

She blushes with delight then nods. She notices the
stitches.

                         GRACIE
               You got quite a few stitches, I see.

Jake looks at his hand.

                         JAKE
               Yes. You were right about my hand.
               The doctor gave me some medicine too,
               but otherwise I'm good.

                         GRACIE
               I am happy it was only the medicine.

                         JAKE
               Uhhhhh, Well... not exactly!(sigh)
               I don't wanna talk about it.

Gracie's laughter fills the room. Jake laughs with her.

                    GRACIE
               (with laughter)
          It is not something to laugh at,
          I know. I am terribly sorry.

Laughter ends. Moment of silence arises between them.

                    GRACIE
          I do not have much to say, Isaac, but
          I am very happy to be here with you.

                    JAKE
          I'm happy too.

They both stare into each other's eyes with delight. After a moment,
she picks up the Bible off the table.

                    GRACIE
          Are you still reading?

                    JAKE
          Oh yes. I'm almost done with
          Epeisians- or is it, Efeshians?

                    GRACIE
          Do you mean Ephesians?

                    JAKE
          Yes, Ephesians. Actually, I do have
          a question for you. May I?

Gracie hands Jake the Bible. He takes it and flips through. Finally,
he scans down the page with his finger.

                    JAKE
          Here it is. It says,
               (Ephesians 2:8-9(KJV))
          "(8) For by grace are ye saved through
          faith; and that not of yourselves: it
          is the gift of God: (9) Not of works,
          lest any man should boast."
               (to Gracie)
          What does that mean?

                    GRACIE
          Do you remember reading in Romans
          that the penalty for sin is death?

                    JAKE
          Yes, I remember.

                    GRACIE
          It says that our good deeds cannot save
          us from going to hell, only God's grace,
          through faith in his son Jesus. It is the
          only way to be saved in God's eyes. Our
          good deeds do not matter, because our
          salvation has nothing to do with us. It is
          a gift from God we need to accept by faith.

                                        (CONTINUED)

                    JAKE
          Explain faith to me.

                    GRACIE
          Faith is believing in something that
          cannot be proven, but you know
          it to be true, so you trust it.

                    JAKE
          Believe in something I can not
          prove. How can anyone do that?

                    GRACIE
          You do not realize it, Isaac, but we all
          it takes live by faith. When you cross a
          bridge, faith to believe that the bridge
          will not collapse on you. You do not even
          ponder it, because you believe that the
          people who built it did a good job. Or
          perhaps you take the bus, you put your
          faith in that bus driver that they will
          take you to your destination safely.
          But both of these examples are blind
          faith, because you do not know who these
          people are, but faith in God is based on
          a personal relationship with him. It is
          not a faith in the unknown.

Moment of silence as Jake takes in her comments.

                    JAKE
          Is love by faith too?

                    GRACIE
          Yes, very much so.

Jake closes the Bible and sets it down on the table. He slowly
slides his hand toward her and takes her hand.

                    JAKE
               (softly)
          Do you love me?

Her emotions awaken. She gazes back at the door.

                    GRACIE
          I should be getting back (sigh)
          before Father knows I am here.

After a moment, Gracie hesitantly pulls back her hand and stands up.
Jake stands and follows her to the door.

                    JAKE
          Do you love me, Gracie?

                    GRACIE
          I very much enjoyed this time
          we shared. Goodnight, Isaac.

Gracie exits the room, closing the door after her. Jake gives a deep
regretful sigh.

                                        (CONTINUED)

                         JAKE
                    I messed up.

He makes his way to the table and takes a seat.

                         JAKE
                    Ughhhh! I messed up bad.

After a moment, he picks up the fork and sees an empty plate.
He stares over at Bark who's happily licking his chops.

93   **EXT. JACOBS' FARM - NIGHT**

Gracie walks up the porch stairs. Half-way up, she abruptly stops and
holds herself as if she's cold. She has a hard time breathing and
sits on the stairs trying to catch her breath. Mr. Jacobs opens the
back kitchen door.

                         MR. JACOBS
                    Oh, there you are, Gracie. Come, we
                    need to say grace.

94   **EXT. JACOBS' FARM/CARRIAGE - MORNING**

Mr. Jacobs sits in the carriage holding on to the driving straps,
while Jake and Abe are in the back.

                         MR. JACOBS
                    What is taking them so long? We
                    will be late for church.

                         ABE
                    Want me to go check, Father?

                         MR. JACOBS
                    Let us give them another minute.
                         (to Jake)
                    Tell me Isaac, do English women
                    take this long to get ready?

                         JAKE
                    I honestly would not know, Sir.

Gracie and Mrs. Jacobs exit the house.

                         MR. JACOBS
                         (to himself)
                    About time!

95   **INT. AMISH CHURCH - DAY**

Father Bishop wraps up a sermon on God's Sacrificial Love.

                         FATHER BISHOP
                    If God's word has touched anyone here
                    today to accept Jesus Christ as their
                    personal savior. You may rise.

                                                      (CONTINUED)

A few people rise, all of them young men and women. The congregation
is filled with joy. After a moment Jake stands too. It becomes
completely silent.

>   FATHER BISHOP
>   You may have a seat, Isaac. This is
>   not for you.

>   JAKE
>   I don't understand. You said anyone.

>   FATHER BISHOP
>   I am truly joyful that you want to
>   follow our Lord Jesus, but this calling
>   is just for us. You may sit.

>   JAKE
>   But I thought we had a deal.

Chief Elder stands up.

>   CHIEF ELDER
>   Our agreement was for out there. Not in
>   here. I thought you were aware that.

>   JAKE
>   But I was under the impression, what
>   happens in here, you take out there.

Jake looks over the congregation. Everyone, including Samuel, Abe,
and Mr. Jacobs stare down at the ground. Jake swallows his defeat.

>   JAKE
>   I understand.

Jake sits back down. A sick smile forms on Caleb's face.

96   **EXT. AMISH CHURCH PREMISES - DAY**

Abe brings a bucket of water and gives it to Mr. Jacobs.

>   ABE
>   Here you go, Father.

>   MR. JACOBS
>   Have you seen Isaac?

>   ABE
>   He said he will walk home today.

Mr. Jacobs swaps out the empty bucket with the full one.

>   MR. JACOBS
>   (to horse)
>   Here you go. Drink up.

He gives the empty bucket to Abe. Abe leaves. Caleb enters.

                                CALEB
                    Greetings, Brother Jacobs. I pray your
                    day is filled with heavenly blessings?

                                MR. JACOBS
                    Yes, indeed. How may I help you,
                    Brother Caleb?

                                CALEB
                    It is not how you can help me, but
                    rather how I can help you! I did some
                    checking on your family history, and it
                    turns out, Brother Jacobs, you are not
                    who we all thought you were. Is this
                    not true?

                                MR. JACOBS
                    And who am I?

                                CALEB
                    Oh, you know.

                                MR. JACOBS
                    I do not know. Enlighten me with
                    your prudent knowledge.

                                CALEB
                    Let us say, you moved here from another
                    small Amish town. Millersburg sound
                    familiar to you? You were shunned by
                    everyone, so you moved here believing you
                    could hide the truth- believing no one
                    would ever find out- but now I know. I
                    know about you, Brother Jacobs.

Mr. Jacobs' goes into panic and anger mode.

                                MR. JACOBS
                    What is it you want, you, you,
                    you... rat?

                                CALEB
                    Ohhhh, hey now! What ever happened
                    to Brother Caleb!?

                                MR. JACOBS
                    Tell me what you want!

                                CALEB
                    You know perfectly what I want.

                                MR. JACOBS
                    If you were the last person on Earth,
                    I would never give her to you. Never!!!

                                CALEB
                    Oh, but you will, or your family will
                    become a shameful disgrace. You will
                    have to pack your belongings and leave,
                    and I am certain that is not your desire.

                                                        (CONTINUED)

                          MR. JACOBS
              You are evil, Caleb. Pure evil.

                          CALEB
              Neither of us is perfect. You have
              your faults, I have mine.

Mrs. Jacobs enters.

                          MRS. JACOBS
              Good day, Brother Caleb.

                          CALEB
                    (to Mr. Jacobs)
              I expect an answer by tomorrow.

Caleb leaves. Mrs. Jacobs senses something is wrong.

                          MRS. JACOBS
              What was that about?

Mr. Jacobs calms his anger and gives a deep regretful sigh.

97   **EXT. AMISH COUNTRY/CARRIAGE - DAY (TRAVELING)**

Mr. Jacobs drives the carriage. Mrs. Jacobs sits beside him. Abe and
Gracie sit in the back. It is silent for a long time.

                          GRACIE
              You did not stand up for Isaac,
              Father, and neither did you, Abe.

                          MRS. JACOBS
                    (with rebuke)
              That is no way to speak to your
              father, Gracie. Apologize!

                          GRACIE
              I will not apologize!

                          MRS. JACOBS
              You will apologize! Do not make me
              ask you again!

                          GRACIE
                    (steadfast)
              I will not apologize, Mother!

                          MR. JACOBS
                    (calmly)
              Gracie may speak freely.

Mrs. Jacobs is awed by his response.

                          MR. JACOBS
              Say what is on your heart.

                         GRACIE
          What kind of people have we become?
          Father, that when someone wants to
          give their life to the Lord, we deny it
          to them? Jesus spoke out against this,
          did he not?
               (Matthew 23:13(KJV))
          "But woe unto you, scribes and Pharisees,
          hypocrites! for ye shut up the kingdom
          of heaven against men: for ye neither
          go in yourselves, neither suffer ye
          them that are entering to go in."

          Isaac needed you and you let him
          stand there by himself.

                         MRS. JACOBS
          Gracie!

                         MR. JACOBS
               (calm)
          No-no, let her finish.

                         GRACIE
          Have we become like the Pharisees,
          that we deny anyone who is not of
          our own, fellowship into the Lord's
          community? Is it not what the Jews
          did to the Gentiles? I understand
          that we have our own rules to live
          by, but I believe that if our rules
          and traditions contradicts the Word,
          then maybe- just maybe, we ought not
          obey them.

                         MR. JACOBS
          Is that all?

                         GRACIE
          There is one other thing I would
          like to say, yes.

Emotional tears begin to flow down Gracie's face.

                         GRACIE
          I confess, without shame, and without
          regret, that I love Isaac. I do not
          care what anyone thinks. I love him,
          and there is nothing anyone can do or
          say to me to stop me from loving him.

Gracie cries on Abe's shoulder. Abe holds her for comfort. Mr. Jacobs
takes Mrs. Jacobs hand and gives a deep sigh of regret.

                         ABE
          I should have said something, Gracie.
          ...I should have said something.

98   **EXT. COUNTRY FIELD/RIVER - DAY**

Sheriff Phil and his son, MARCUS, a black kid in his early teens,
walk toward the river.

>   MARCUS
>   I'm gonna catch a monster fish
>   today. You'll see, Daddy.

>   SHERIFF PHIL
>   Not if one catches you first.

Sheriff Phil acts like he's the fish catching his son.

>   MARCUS
>   Hey, Daddy! What's that over there?

Sheriff Phil notices an odd glare in the water.

>   SHERIFF PHIL
>   Marcus, why don't you go ahead and
>   set up the gear. I'll be right back.

99   **INT. JACOBS' HOUSE/GRACIE'S ROOM - NIGHT**

It's raining heavily. Gracie looks out the window and sighs with
grief. Mrs. Jacobs enters.

>   MRS. JACOBS
>   Have you seen your father?

Gracie shakes her head and sighs once again.

>   MRS. JACOBS
>   He will return, my beautiful daughter.
>   Do not grieve.

>   GRACIE
>   How do you know?

>   MRS. JACOBS
>   True love always returns. Always!

She gives her a kiss on the forehead. Gracie ponders for a moment
and nods with a slight smile on her face.

100 **EXT. JACOBS' HOUSE/FRONT PORCH - NIGHT**

Rain continues. Mr. Jacobs stands on a porch looking up at the
heavens, with grief on his face.

>   MR. JACOBS
>   Lord. I have given you my heart; my
>   whole life is yours. Why this, Lord?
>   After all these years. Why now?

Mrs. Jacobs comes to him.

(CONTINUED)

                    MRS. JACOBS
          How is my sweet love?

He turns to face her.

                    MRS. JACOBS
          Oh my! What is this sadness I
          see on your face?

                    MR. JACOBS
          Caleb knows, Leah.

                    MRS. JACOBS
          What are you saying?

                    MR. JACOBS
          He knows. He knows about us.

                    MRS. JACOBS
          You mean--

                    MR. JACOBS
          Yes.

                    MRS. JACOBS
          Oh my! How did he find out?

                    MR. JACOBS
          I do not know.

          MRS. JACOBS

          And what does he want?

                    MR. JACOBS
          He wants Gracie, or he will confess
          it to everyone.

Tears of sadness begin to flow down her face.

                    MRS. JACOBS
          I would rather die a hundred deaths than
          surrender our daughter to that unworthy
          man. Never! I will not let you!

                    MR. JACOBS
          I must, Leah. If I do not, everyone will
          know about us. Our children will be
          shamed forever. They will never be able
          to forgive us. We will have to live like
          the English for the rest of our lives.

                    MRS. JACOBS
          Then so be it! We will live like
          the English. Anything but that
          treachery in our home.

                    MR. JACOBS
          I do not want him as a son, but just
          think of Ella and Samuel, and their
                    (MORE)

                         MR. JACOBS(cont'd)
                    arriving baby. Do we truly want
                    to shame them with this? What about
                    Abe and Gracie? This, this life, this
                    is all they know. If we go to the
                    English, what will become of them?
                    What will become of us?

                         MRS. JACOBS
                    Gracie told you she loves Isaac.
                    How can we do this to her?

Mr. Jacobs gives off a deep sorrowful sigh.

                         MR. JACOBS
                    I wish I knew what to do, Leah, but
                    I do not know.

Mrs. Jacobs makes her way to the bench and cries softly. Mr. Jacobs
takes a seat beside her and holds her for comfort.

                         MR. JACOBS
                    Oh, my love!

                         MRS. JACOBS
                    This is not right, Mr. Jacobs...
                    Not right at all.

101   **INT. JACOBS' BARN/JAKE'S ROOM - NIGHT**

We hear rain pounding the roof. Jake enters and sits at the table
completely drenched. Bark comes to him and whines.

DOOR: KNOCK-KNOCK!

                         JAKE
                    Yes.

                         GRACIE
                    It is I, Gracie.

Jake makes his way to the door and opens it. Gracie bursts through
and immediately embraces him with tears in her eyes.

                         GRACIE
                    I was worried sick, Isaac.

She sighs.

                         GRACIE
                    Where did you go?

Jake is hesitant to hold her, but after moment, he gives in and holds
her tightly with love.

                         JAKE
                    I didn't mean to hurt you.

Moment of silence as they hold each other.

                                                    (CONTINUED)

                         GRACIE
              I was deeply grieved what happened at
              church. I desperately wanted someone
              to stand up for you, but nobody did.

                         JAKE
              Things are the way they are. We
              cannot change them.

Gracie ends the embrace.

                         GRACIE
              Did you mean it, accepting Jesus
              as your personal savior?

                         JAKE
              I did it for you, Gracie, because
              I love you.

Gracie, with sadness on her face, walks a little further away with
her back toward Jake.

                         GRACIE
              Then you did not do it for yourself.

Jake walks up to her.

                         JAKE
              I'd give anything- Anything and
              everything to be with you!

Moment of silence. Gracie turns to him.

                         GRACIE
              Giving your life to Jesus is a decision
              you must make alone, Isaac. You cannot
              do it for me, nor anyone else. That is how
              salvation in Jesus Christ works.

Jake gives a deep sigh.

                         JAKE
              Yes, I understand.

Gracie embraces Jake once again.

                         GRACIE
              I am so glad you did not abandon us,
              Isaac. I was deeply afraid you left.

                         JAKE
              I'd never abandon you. Never-ever,
              I swear it!

Gracie sighs. Moment of silence as they continue to hold one another.
Gracie ends the embrace and whispers to him.

                         GRACIE
              I want to show you something.

Jake whispers back to her.

                                                    (CONTINUED)

                                    JAKE
                    What?

                                    GRACIE
                    You must not confess it to anyone,
                    or I will be shamed for life.

Jake looks around in confusion.

                                    GRACIE
                    Promise me. (deep sigh)

Confused, Jake nods. Gracie walks off a tad with her back toward him.
She sighs with emotion as she ponders for a bit.

********************************SLOW MOTION*******************************

She hesitantly slides off her head covering. Long graceful wavy hair
flows down to her waist.

*****************************BACK TO NORMAL*****************************

She turns toward him and sighs deeply. Jake swallows his emotions as
he gazes at her enchanting beauty with awe and wonder. He approaches
her and looks directly into her eyes.

                                    JAKE
                        (softly)
                    There is nothing on Earth more
                    beautiful than you.

After a moment, he kisses her on the forehead and embraces her
tightly, as if they're glued to one another for life.

102   **EXT. MT. JOY HARDWARE STORE - DAY**

        Jake and Abe load the carriage with a fence. Sheriff Phil pulls the
        police car alongside them.

        POLICE SIREN: EEEUUUUU-EEEUUUUU!

        The driver's side window rolls down.

                                    SHERIFF PHIL
                        (to Jake)
                    Just the man I wanted to see.

103   **EXT. COUNTRY FIELD/RIVER - DAY**

        Jake's Porsche is pulled out of the river as Sheriff Phil pulls in
        with the police car.

                                    SHERIFF PHIL(O.S.)
                    It was lodged between two huge>>>

104   **EXT. COUNTRY FIELD/RIVER - DAY (LATER)**

                    SHERIFF PHIL
            >>>rocks. That is why we had such a
            hard time locating it.

Jake and Sheriff Phil circle around to the back of the car.

                    SHERIFF PHIL
            "JK D ICE"

                    JAKE
            This car seems expensive. You
            sure it's mine?

                    SHERIFF PHIL
            Car matches Gracie's description.
            It has to be yours.

Jake opens the door. Water gushes out, along with two bouncing fish.

                    SHERIFF PHIL
            I know what I'm having for lunch.

Jake opens the glove compartment and scours through. Sheriff Phil
takes a peek inside.

                    SHERIFF PHIL
            Leather heated seats, Built-in
            GPS, push button starting. It's
            a shame this piece of art is now
            a piece of junk.

                    JAKE
            There's nothing here.

                    SHERIFF PHIL
            Try the arm rest.

Jake opens the arm rest and finds a wallet.

                    JAKE
            I found something.

Jake gets out of the car, opens the wallet, and finds his driver's
license picture staring up at him.

                    SHERIFF PHIL
            You hit the jackpot, my Amish friend.

                    JAKE
            My name is Jake Daniels, and I live
            in Pittsburgh.

                    SHERIFF PHIL
            I guess your journey ends here, huh?

                    JAKE
                (with sadness)
            Yeah, I guess it does.

(CONTINUED)

As Jake continues looking through the wallet, a key falls on the floor. Jake picks it up.

                    JAKE
          This must be my house key.

Sheriff Phil takes it from him. "147" is etched in.

                    SHERIFF PHIL
          Looks like some sort of locker key to me.

                    JAKE
          Locker key?

                    SHERIFF PHIL
          That's what I think.

He hands it back to Jake.

                    SHERIFF PHIL
          What you gonna do about Gracie?

                    JAKE
          How do you know about us?

                    SHERIFF PHIL
          Let's just say I have my sources.

                    JAKE
          I don't know. I've gotten used to this
          place, this life. I wouldn't mind living
          here, if I could.

                    SHERIFF PHIL
          My first thoughts are, you will not
          be welcomed into their community,
          doesn't matter how hard you try.
          Then again, you managed to get this
          far, so not really sure what to say.

Jake ponders for a moment and sighs.

105   **EXT. JACOBS' FARM/FIELD - DAY**

Jake and Abe repair a section of a fence. Suddenly, Bark stares in a
certain direction and growls.

A buggy enters the driveway of Mr. Jacobs' farm.

                    ABE
          It's Caleb and his father.

                    JAKE
          How do you know?

                    ABE
          The buggy and horse are theirs.

106   **INT. JACOBS' HOUSE/KITCHEN - DAY**

Mr. Jacobs, Mrs. Jacobs, Caleb, and CALEB'S FATHER, an Amish man
in his 40's, are sitting around the kitchen table.

                    CALEB'S FATHER
          What say you, Brother Jacobs?

Mrs. Jacobs leaves the room crying.

107   **INT. JACOBS' BARN/JAKE'S ROOM - NIGHT**

Jake drinks another pill, picks up Gracie's Bible, and makes his
way to the bed.

DOOR: KNOCK-KNOCK!

                    JAKE
          It's open.

Mr. Jacobs enters.

                    MR. JACOBS
          Hello, Isaac.

                    JAKE
          Hello, Mr. Jacobs. What brings you
          here at this late hour?

                    MR. JACOBS
          Is that Gracie's Bible?

                    JAKE
          Yes Sir. She lent it to me during
          my stay.

Mr. Jacobs gives a deep sigh.

                    MR. JACOBS
          I understand that your car
          has been found.

                    JAKE
          Yes, yes it has.

                    MR. JACOBS
          Did you find what you needed
          to get yourself home?

                    JAKE
          I did.

Mr. Jacobs walks around for a tad and gives a deep sigh.

                    MR. JACOBS
          I know that you are fond of my daughter,
          Isaac- I know that, so what I am about
          to say may not sit well with you.

Apprehension forms on Jake's face.

(CONTINUED)

                         MR. JACOBS
              I have given Gracie into marriage.

Moment of silence as Jake takes in the grieving news.

                         JAKE
              May I ask who?

                         MR. JACOBS
              Does it matter who?

                         JAKE
              It's Caleb. Isn't it?

                         MR. JACOBS
              It does not matter, Isaac.

                         JAKE
              It matters to me.

                         MR. JACOBS
              Why does it matter?

                         JAKE
              Because I love her, and I know she
              loves me too.

                         MR. JACOBS
              Has Gracie confessed her love to you?

Jake swallows with guilt.

                         JAKE
              Well no... not by mouth, but I know it.
              I know it by faith.

Moment of silence as neither of them know what to say.

                         MR. JACOBS
              I want to thank you for all the hard
              work you have done for my family. Mrs.
              Jacobs and I greatly appreciate it, but...
              (sigh) I do not know how to say this.

                         JAKE
              But I need to go.

                         MR. JACOBS
              It is for the best, yes.

                         JAKE
              I see.

                         MR. JACOBS
              I am not requiring you to leave the
              community, Isaac. I am sure Samuel
              would be very content to have you back.

Jake nods.

                                                        (CONTINUED)

                    JAKE
          I lost what I love most to a man that does
          not deserve her. It would utterly break
          my heart to stay and see them together.

Mr. Jacobs gives a deep sigh.

                    MR. JACOBS
          Things are different here, Isaac. I do
          not expect you to understand our ways.

                    JAKE
          You're right, Mr. Jacobs. I don't
          understand- I don't understand it at all,
          and here's why I don't understand it.
          You see I've been reading this book>>>

Jake holds up Gracie's Bible.

                    JAKE
          >>>and one thing I've learned is that
          you can't force love on anyone. Love
          is a personal choice, and yet she did
          not have any choice in the matter.

                    MR. JACOBS
          We do not choose husbands for our
          daughters based on love. You should
          have realized that by now.

                    JAKE
          If it's not love, then what's it
          based on? Personal interest?

Mr. Jacobs ponders with regret and gives a sigh.

                    MR. JACOBS
          I did what I had to do, not what I
          wished to do. Let us leave it at that.
          How much more do I owe for your work?

                    JAKE
          You don't owe me anything, Mr. Jacobs.
          What I did, I did not do for you.

                    MR. JACOBS
          Very well... I will have Abe take you
          to the bus station in the morning. I am
          sorry to see you go. Your presence will be
          missed. Be blessed on your journey home.

Mr. Jacobs walks to the door. He's just about to exit.

                    JAKE
          May I say goodbye to her before I go?

Mr. Jacobs gives a deep regretful sigh.

                    MR. JACOBS
          She is engaged to another, Isaac.
          I could never permit such a thing.

(CONTINUED)

Jake nods with grief. Bark wines.

> JAKE
> One last favor. I beg you.

> MR. JACOBS
> Speak.

> JAKE
> I'd like to take Bark with me.

Bark strolls over to Mr. Jacobs and whines slightly. Mr. Jacobs rubs the dogs head.

> MR. JACOBS
> He is yours.

Mr. Jacobs is about to exit, but stops to ponder.

> MR. JACOBS
> A short note. Please keep it short.

Mr. Jacobs exits. Heartbroken, Jake takes a seat at the table. Bark places his head on Jake's lap and whines.

108   **INT. JACOBS' BARN/JAKE'S ROOM - DAWN**

Wearing his city clothes, Jake sleeps with his head on the table. A flower lays on top of Gracie's Bible, with a folded note underneath.

DOOR: KNOCK-KNOCK!

Bark and Jake wake up.

109   **INT/EXT. COUNTRY ROAD - JACOBS' BUGGY - NIGHT (TRAVELING)**

It is just before dawn. Abe drives the buggy. Jake and Bark are the passengers. A mood of utter sadness fills the air.

110   **EXT. BUS STATION - DAWN**

Abe pulls the buggy beside the bus station. Jake gets out.

> ABE
> (to Bark)
> You will be missed, my old friend.

Abe hugs Bark. Bark whines. Jake puts out his hand.

> JAKE
> You are like a brother to me, Abe.

Teary eyed, Abe gets off the buggy and hugs him tightly.

> ABE
> Brothers for life.

111   **INT. JACOBS' HOUSE/KITCHEN - DAY**

Mrs. Jacobs works the kitchen. Mr. Jacobs takes a seat at the table.

>   MRS. JACOBS
>   You have to tell her.

>   MR. JACOBS
>   I will.

>   MRS. JACOBS
>   When?

He picks up the newspaper.

>   MR. JACOBS
>   Soon.

>   MRS. JACOBS
>   How soon?

>   MR. JACOBS
>   I do not know. Soon!

With frustration, Mrs. Jacobs goes to him and takes away the
newspaper and slams it on the table.

>   MRS. JACOBS
>   You will tell her, NOW!!!

Gracie happily strolls into the kitchen.

>   GRACIE
>   Good morning Father, Mother. Tell
>   me what?

>   MRS. JACOBS
>   Please have a seat, Gracie.

>   MR. JACOBS
>   Not now.

>   MRS. JACOBS
>   Now, Mr. Jacobs!

Gracie takes a seat across from them. Mr. Jacobs gives a deep sigh.
He doesn't know how to begin.

>   MRS. JACOBS
>   Fine! I will do it.
>   (to Gracie)
>   Caleb's father visited us yesterday.

>   GRACIE
>   And what did he want?

>   MR. JACOBS
>   And... You know.

(CONTINUED)

                              GRACIE
                         (with confusion)
                    Know what, Father?

                              MR. JACOBS
                         (different intonation)
                    You know.

Moment of silence as Gracie suspects what he's referring to.

                              GRACIE
                    You don't mean?

                              MRS. JACOBS
                    Yes.

                              GRACIE
                    And you did not accept, did you?

Mr. Jacobs and Mrs. Jacobs look at each other with shame.

                              GRACIE
                    Please tell me you did not accept.

Mr. Jacobs gives off a deep sigh of regret.

                              GRACIE
                         (Softer to Louder)
                    No!... No! Why would you do that, Father?
                    Why? You know I hate that man! I hate
                    him with the utmost passion! HOW COULD
                    YOU, FATHER?! HOW COULD YOU?!

She storms out of the kitchen.

112   **EXT. JACOBS' FARM - DAY**

Gracie storms out of the house desperately looking for Jake.

                              GRACIE
                    ISAAC!... ISAAC!

113   **INT. JACOBS' BARN - DAY**

Gracie runs into the barn and checks all the stalls.

                              GRACIE
                    ISAAC, WHERE ARE YOU???

114   **INT. JACOBS' BARN/JAKE'S ROOM - DAY**

Gracie knocks on Jake's door with utter grief in her voice.

                              GRACIE(O.S.)
                    ISAAC!!!

She knocks again.

                                GRACIE(O.S.)
                        IT IS I, GRACIE!!!

She enters and sees Jake's work clothes neatly folded on the bed.
She makes her way to the bed and picks up the clothes. She takes
a whiff. She spots the red flower on the Bible with the note
underneath the flower. She quickly pulls out the note.

                                JAKE(V.O.)
                           (Jake's note)
                        *"Gracie- my lovely angel,
                        I am deeply grieved that I must
                        leave without saying goodbye."*

                                GRACIE
                        Oh no.

Gracie quickly sits on the bed and tries to catch her breath.

                                GRACIE
                        Please, no.

She continues reading.

                                JAKE(V.O.)
                           (Jake's note)
                        *"This note is all I could do. I want you
                        to know that you are the kindest and
                        most beautiful person I have ever come
                        to know, and I know I will never find
                        anyone kinder and more beautiful than
                        you. I've loved you from the moment I
                        opened my eyes, and will love you till
                        the day my eyes close on this earth. I
                        desperately wish things could have
                        turned out differently, but I guess we
                        cannot always have everything we want in
                        life. Keep me in your silent prayers.*

                        With my deepest love, Isaac."

Gracie takes a hold of Jake's pillow and hugs it tightly, as she
grieves her heart out. Moments later, the buggy is heard pulling
into the driveway. She quickly gets up and leaves.

115   **EXT. JACOBS' FARM - DAY**

Abe pulls the buggy in front of the barn. Gracie exits the barn
and runs to him, grabbing him by the shirt with anger.

                                GRACIE
                        WHERE IS ISAAC??? TELL ME!!!

                                ABE
                        I took him to town.

                                GRACIE
                        WHY!?

                              ABE
                    He is going home.

                              GRACIE
                    AND DID YOU NOT THINK I WANTED TO
                    SAY GOODBYE!? WHY WOULD YOU DO
                    THAT, ABE!? WHY!? TELL ME!!!

          Gracie falls to the ground and cries out her broken heart.

                              GRACIE
                    Why didn't you tell me, Abe? You knew I
                    loved him. Why didn't you say anything?

          Sorrow and compassion forms on his face. Moment of silence as
          Gracie continues to grieve.

                              ABE
                    Get up!

          Abe tries to pull her up by the arm.

                              ABE
                    Get up, Gracie! The bus leaves at 8.
                    We can still catch him.

116   **EXT. COUNTRY ROAD - DAY (TRAVELING)**

          A FRENCH BIKER, dressed in biking gear from head to toe, rides
          his bike on the side of the street. Jacobs' carriage zooms by
          engulfing the biker with dust, completely.

                              FRENCH BIKER
                    SACRA BLEU!

          He coughs his lungs out.

117   **EXT. COUNTRY ROAD - DAY (TRAVELING)**

          Abe drives the buggy wildly. Gracie is the passenger.

                              ABE
                         (to horse)
                    HYAAAAAA!

                              GRACIE
                    We are not going to make it.

                              ABE
                    HYAAAAAA! We have to make it.

118   **INT. PASSENGER BUS - DAY**

          Jake sits on a bus seat with Bark at his side. BUS TRAVELER, a man
          in his 50's, sits directly across from Jake, on the opposite side
          of the isle.

                                                              (CONTINUED)

>   BUS DRIVER(V.O.)
>   (overhead speaker)
>   Please make your final adjustments.
>   We will be leaving shortly.

A teardrop slides down Jake's face. Bark lays his head on
his lap. Jake pets him.

119   **EXT. JACOBS' CARRIAGE - DAY (TRAVELING)**

Abe continues to push the horse to its limits.

>   GRACIE
>   Please God! I beg you!

He brings the buggy to a halt just as the bus wheels begin
to roll out. Gracie jumps out and runs after the bus.

>   GRACIE
>   ISAAC!!!

She runs on the side of the bus.

>   GRACIE
>   ISAAC, DO NOT LEAVE!!!

120   **INT. PASSENGER BUS - DAY (TRAVELING)**

Bark raises his head, moves around his ears, and barks.

>   JAKE
>   What's wrong?

121   **EXT. MT. JOY BUS STATION - DAY**

Gracie runs as hard as she possibly can, but the bus pulls
further and further away.

>   GRACIE
>   I LOVE YOU, ISAAC!!! I LOVE YOU!!!

Exhausted, she falls to her knees and cries her heart out.

122   **INT. PASSENGER BUS - DAY (TRAVELING)**

Bark continues barking.

>   JAKE
>   What is it?

>   BUS TRAVELER
>   Hey! Do you mind telling your mutt
>   to shut up?

>   JAKE
>   Easy boy. Easy.

Bark puts his head back down and whines.

VOCAL FAITH SONG BEGINS...

123   **TRANSITION MONTAGE**

We see superimposed shots of the wonderful memories Jake and Gracie shared between themselves when they were together.

VOCAL FAITH SONG ENDS.

FADE OUT:

===

===

INTERMISSION

===

===

FADE IN:

124   **EXT. RITZY HIGH-RISE - NIGHT**

A yellow taxicab pulls in front of Jake's luxurious high-rise building complex.

125   **INT. TAXICAB - NIGHT**

Jake and Bark are in the back of a taxicab. CAB DRIVER, a Hippie looking man, in his 40's, presses the mileage machine.

                    CAB DRIVER
          That is it, yo. 645 Pittsburgh Ave.

                    JAKE
          Is this where I live?

                    CAB DRIVER
          How should I know? You told me to
          bring you here and I did.

                    JAKE
          Right... How much do I owe you?

                    CAB DRIVER
          That'll be $45. Cash or credit?

Jake gives him a $50 bill.

                    JAKE
          Keep the change.

126   **INT. RITZY HIGH-RISE/FRONT GATE - NIGHT**

Jake and Bark exit the cab. TWO SIDEWALK GIRLS(in their 20's) pass by, checking him out with flirtatious glances.

>   SIDEWALK GIRL
>   Like your dog.

>   JAKE
>   Thanks.

They giggle between themselves. Jake approaches the front gate. A "NO PETS ALLOWED" sign stares at him.

>   JAKE
>   (to Bark)
>   Guess you'll be sleeping outside.

Bark whines a bit.

>   JAKE
>   Only kidding.

He pulls the gate, but it's locked. He takes out the "147" key from his wallet and tries to stick it in, but it won't fit. Jake sees the sign with an arrow "PRESS HERE FOR HELP," He presses the button. The Swedish accent lady answers.

>   SWEDISH GIRL(V.O.)
>   Welcome to Bella Towers. How may I
>   help you?

>   JAKE
>   Yes, Hi. I think I live here, but I
>   seem to have lost my key.

>   SWEDISH GIRL(V.O.)
>   Why don't you use the scanner?

>   JAKE
>   Scanner? I don't see- Oh, never mind!

Jake places his hand on the scanner. A green laser beam scans his hand from top to bottom. The gate opens immediately.

>   SWEDISH GIRL(V.O.)
>   Welcome home, Mr. Daniels.

>   JAKE
>   Thanks.

>   SWEDISH GIRL(V.O.)
>   Come to the front desk and I'll
>   have another key ready for you.

>   JAKE
>   Will do.
>   (to Bark)
>   Hide under this bush till I find a
>   way to get you in.

Bark does so.

127   **INT. RITZY HIGH-RISE/FRONT DESK - NIGHT**

A gorgeous SWEDISH GIRL(in her 30's) with a sweet accent works the
front desk. Jake approaches her.

>   SWEDISH GIRL
>   I have your key right here, Mr. Daniels.

She hands him a card key.

>   JAKE
>   (confused)
>   What's this?

>   SWEDISH GIRL
>   The key to your apartment, Mr. Daniels.

>   JAKE
>   Oh right! Sorry, I had a long day.

>   SWEDISH GIRL
>   I understand. Let me check your
>   mailbox while you are here.

As she checks, Jake eyes the box where she pulls the mail from, and
sees, *"Jake Daniels - Room 720."*

>   SWEDISH GIRL
>   Yes, there's quite a lot mail.

As she hands him the mail, a pen slides out and lands directly on the
desk. She grabs it and hands it to him.

>   SWEDISH GIRL
>   Someone left this for you.

Jake takes the pen and checks it out. He sees the initials "JTID"
etched in. He pulls the note inserted into the clip.

CHORK'S NOTE: *"Hope you're doing well. Chork :)"*

>   JAKE
>   Know anyone by the name of Chork?

>   SWEDISH GIRL
>   No. I'm afraid I do not. Sorry.

He takes a step to leave. Mikey, Jake's neighbor, walks in.

>   MIKEY
>   Hey Jakey, my Bro!

Mikey fake karate chops him.

>   MIKEY
>   Where have you been all this time?
>   I almost thought you got whacked.

>   JAKE
>   (with straight face)
>   I'm still here.

(CONTINUED)

Jake walks off leaving Mikey hanging.

                         MIKEY
                    (to Swedish Girl)
               What's up with him?

128   **EXT. RITZY HIGH-RISE/FRONT GATE - NIGHT**

Bark hears a whistle and takes off.

129   **EXT. RITZY HIGH-RISE/BACK ALLEY DOOR - NIGHT**

Jake whistles again. Bark barks as he enters.

                         JAKE
               Shhhhhhhhh.

130   **INT. RITZY HIGH-RISE/JAKE'S APARTMENT - NIGHT**

Jake opens the door to his apartment and turns on the lights. The
apartment is dusty, cold, and void of life.

                         JAKE
               Is this really my place?

He walks around and checks out the paintings, ending with his last
creation; the one he stuck the holes in the eyes.

                         JAKE
               Freaky.

Jake notices the signature. He grabs a pen and paper and signs his
name. He compares the signatures. They match.

                         JAKE
               Freaky is right.

131   **INT. RITZY HIGH-RISE/JAKE'S BATHROOM - NIGHT**

Jake turns off the shower, puts a towel around his waist, and goes
to the steamed-up mirror. He wipes the condensation with his hand.
His reflection stares back at him.

                         JAKE
               Who are you, Jake Daniels?

VOCAL FAITH SONG BEGINS...

132   **INT. RITZY HIGH-RISE/JAKE'S APARTMENT - NIGHT (MONTAGE)**

We see an all-night montage of JAKE scouring through the things in
his apartment trying to find out who he is.

133   **INT. RITZY HIGH-RISE/JAKE'S BEDROOM - MORNING**

Bark licks Jake's face as he lays asleep on the floor. An assortment
of photos and papers are scattered all around him.

VOCAL FAITH SONG ENDS.

                    JAKE
          Ugh, Bark! I told you that's gross.

He wipes his face with his arm. Bark barks.

                    JAKE
          Shhhhh! You wanna sleep outside!?

Bark whines.

                    JAKE
          Alright then.

Moment of silence.

                    JAKE
          I went through this all stuff and
          it looks like I worked for some
          security company.

               (to himself)
          What was that name?

He searches through some papers and picks up a check stub.

                    JAKE
          Morrison Securities. Probably as a
          security guard.

Jake shows Bark a picture of him and Gina.

                    JAKE
          This might be my girlfriend, or it used
          to be, not really sure. What you think?

Bark growls at the picture.

                    JAKE
          Yeah, me too. And check this out, an
          envelope loaded with cash. There must be
          like $5,000 in here... I couldn't find
          anything on my parents. Not sure why.

134   **INT. RITZY HIGH-RISE/JAKE'S KITCHEN - MORNING**

He opens the fridge and it's completely empty.

                    JAKE
          Of course.

He sees a pair of car keys on the table.

                    JAKE
          C'mon, I'm starving.

135   **INT. RITZY HIGH-RISE/GARAGE COMPLEX - MORNING**

A blinking red light emanates from a small black box. Camera pulls out from the box to reveal it's stuck underneath a Luxurious Audi SUV. Jake and Bark walk into the garage.

CAR ALARM: CHIRP-CHIRP!

The tail-lights blink on the Luxurious Audi SUV.

> JAKE
> (to Bark)
> What do you think of my buggy?
> Pretty spiffy, huh?

Jake opens the door. Bark jumps right in.

136   **EXT. HOTDOG STAND - DAY**

Jake, with Bark at his side, approach a hotdog stand with a sign, "Molly's Dogs - Best Hotdogs in Pittsburgh." HOTDOG SERVER, a female in her 60's, serves him.

> HOTDOG SERVER
> What can I get you, Sonny?

> JAKE
> I'll take 2 hotdogs.

Bark barks.

> JAKE
> Make that 4.

Moment of silence as the server prepares the hotdogs.

> HOTDOG SERVER
> You look familiar. Haven't I seen
> you somewhere before?

> JAKE
> Jake Daniels is my name. Sound familiar?

> HOTDOG SERVER
> Naaa, I'm not good with names, but I'm
> certain I have seen you before, just
> can't remember where.

She hands him the hotdogs.

> HOTDOG SERVER
> That'll be $12.

Jake gives her a $50 bill.

> HOTDOG SERVER
> I'm sorry, but it's too early in the day
> to break a $50. Do you have anything smaller?

(CONTINUED)

                          JAKE
                That's okay. Keep it.

                          HOTDOG SERVER
                You sure!?

                          JAKE
                It's only money. Keep it.

                          HOTDOG SERVER
                God Bless You, Sonny! Come back anytime!

137   **EXT. HOTDOG STAND/FURTHER AWAY - DAY (LATER)**

Jake sits at a table eating his hotdogs. Hotdog stand visible in the
background. Bark swallows his hotdogs in a few bites then stares over
at Jake's hotdogs, and whines.

                          JAKE
                Hey, now! These are mine.

Bark whines some more and licks his chops.

                          JAKE
                Okay. I'll get you more when I'm done.

He looks across the street and sees a high-rise with "MORRISON
SECURITIES" on it. He pulls out the check stub from his pocket. The
logos are identical.

138   **INT. MORRISON SECURITIES BUILDING - DAY**

We pull out from a *Morrison Securities* sign written on the wall, to
reveal MORRISON'S SECRETARY, a lady in her 40's, sitting in front of
a computer, typing. Jake walks out of the elevator and goes to her.

                          MORRISON'S SECRETARY
                May I help you?

                          JAKE
                I believe I work here, at least I
                did. Jake Daniels is the name.

                          MORRISON'S SECRETARY
                I've been with this company since it opened
                and I've never seen you here before. You sure
                you have the right place?

Jake gives her the check stub.

                          JAKE
                Is this you?

                          MORRISON'S SECRETARY
                That's our check stubs, yes.

139 **INT. MORRISON SECURITIES BUILDING/OFFICE - DAY**

Morrison Securities President, MR. MORRISON, a plump, toupee wearing, white man in his 50's, dressed business casual, watches a martial arts fight on a huge Plasma TV.

DESK PHONE: RING-RING!

He pauses the fight and answers on speakerphone.

>   MR. MORRISON
>   I'm busy.

>   MORRISON'S SECRETARY(V.O.)
>   There's a gentleman here who says
>   he works for you.

>   MR. MORRISON
>   What's his name?

>   MORRISON'S SECRETARY(V.O.)
>   Jake Daniels.

Instant panic forms on his face. He gets up from his chair and paces around nervously.

>   MORRISON'S SECRETARY(V.O.)
>   Hello? Mr. Morrison?

>   MR. MORRISON
>   Ask him what he wants?

We hear some mumbling on the phone.

>   MORRISON'S SECRETARY(V.O.)
>   He wants his job back.

>   MR. MORRISON
>   Tell him we're not hiring right now.

He nervously picks up the receiver and dials.

>   MR. MORRISON
>   Pick-up! Pick-up!

>   MYSTERIOUS PERSON(V.O.)
>   (on phone)
>   Yeah.

>   MR. MORRISON
>   (irritated)
>   Daniels is outside my door asking
>   questions. I thought we had a deal. No
>   fighters ever come to the office. Ever!!!

>   MYSTERIOUS PERSON(V.O.)
>   (on phone)
>   Relax, Mr. Morrison. Drink your
>   latte, smoke your cigar.>>>

140   **INT. NIGHT CLUB/OFFICE - DAY**

                         MYSTERIOUS PERSON
                    >>>We'll quickly take care of this
                    little nuisance.

The Mysterious Man hangs up his cell.

141   **INT. NIGHT CLUB/DANCE FLOOR ---> BOSS' OFFICE - DAY**

We follow the back of Mysterious Man as he walks by the dance floor
making his way down the basement stairs. He enters the basement and
passes by the ring. He finally ends up in front of Boss' office.

142   **INT. NIGHT CLUB/BOSS' OFFICE - DAY**

Chork enters Boss' office.

                         CHORK
                    Guess who's back?

143   **INT. JAKE'S AUDI SUV - DAY**

Jake gets into his SUV. Bark sits on the passenger's seat.

                         JAKE
                    No luck.

144   **EXT. PITTSBURGH ROAD - DAY**

Jake pulls up to a red light. Bark is the passenger. A road
construction crew puts up some road blocks. Jake's forced to take a
detour into an alley.

145   **EXT. DARK ALLEY - DAY**

Suddenly, Jake's SUV gets hit from behind by a Hummer with tinted
windows. Jake pulls over and goes to check on the driver.

                         JAKE
                    Are you alright?

The front window rolls down a tad and gun is pointed at him.

                         CHORK
                    Don't move, Jake.

                         JAKE
                    Who are you, and how do you know me?

Suddenly, 6 ASIAN GUYS, jump out of the car, and surround him.

146   **INT. JAKE'S AUDI SUV - DAY**

Bark viciously tries to break out of the car.

147   **EXT. DARK ALLEY - DAY**

The 6 ASIAN GUYS attack JAKE; martial arts style. Jake tries to fight
them off.

148   **INT. JAKE'S AUDI SUV - DAY**

Bark shoves his might into a window and cracks it.

149   **EXT. DARK ALLEY - DAY**

Outnumbered 6 to 1, Jake doesn't stand a chance. They bring him down
to the ground. Chork gets out of the car. GANG GUY #3 and GANG GUY #4
raise him to his knees.

                    CHORK
          Jake, Jake, Jake... What am I going to
          do with you, huh? After all that we've
          been through together, you thought you
          could pull a fast one on us, aye?

                    JAKE
          Who are you?

                    CHORK
          Oh, so you don't remember me. Is
          that it? Maybe THIS>>>

Chork punches him in the stomach.

                    CHORK
          >>>will unclog your memory. WHERE'S
          THE MONEY!?

Jake coughs hard.

                    JAKE
          You're confusing me with someone else.

                    CHORK
          Oh, so you like playing stupid.

Chork hits him again in the stomach.

                    CHORK
          WHERE'S THE MONEY, YOU PILE OF
          DOG WASTE!!!

He coughs even harder.

                    JAKE
          I've got amnesia. I don't know anything.

                    CHORK
              (to gang)
          Will you listen to this guy? He's
          got amnesia. How convenient of him.

(CONTINUED)

Chork grabs Jake by his hair and pulls back.

                    CHORK
          Do you take us for morons? Do you?

Chork hits him again a third time. Jake coughs up blood.

                    JAKE
          Please, I'll get you your money.
          Just let me go.

                    CHORK
               (to Gang Guy #1)
          I'm tired of listening to his lies.
          Put him out of his misery.

Gang Guy #3 and #4 drops Jake to the ground. GANG GUY #1 pulls out
his gun.

                    CHORK
          No-no. Give him the "nice and easy"
          treatment. He earned it.

                    GANG GUY #1
               (with pleasure)
          "Nice and easy" is my favorite.
               (to Gang Guy #2)
          Here, hold my gun.

Gang Guy #1 hands his gun to GANG GUY #2, and goes to Jake.

                    JAKE
          Give me another chance. I'll make
          things right, I swear!

                    GANG GUY #1
          Too late for that.

He roughs up Jake for a few seconds, when suddenly, Bark
breaks through the window and dives on him with fierce anger.

                    GANG GUY #1
          AHHHHH! HELP ME! HELP ME!

Chork tries to shoot Bark, but misses. Bark maims the guy
pretty good.

                    CHORK
               (to Gang Guy #1)
          Stop moving, numskull.

Bark quickly dives on Chork, knocking the gun from his hand.

                    CHORK
          AHHHHH! GET'M OFF!

Gang Guy #2 tries to shoot Bark a few times, but misses.

                    CHORK
          AHHHHHHHH! GET'M OFF! GET'M OFF!

After a few more tries, he finally shoots Bark. The bullet goes
through the dog and hits Chork in the shoulder.

                    JAKE
          NOOOOOOOOOOOOOOOOOOOOOO!!!

Chork pushes the dog off himself and places his hand on the wound.
Blood sticks to his hand.

                    CHORK
          You shot me, you moron!

                    GANG GUY #2
          But I wasn't aiming at you.

                    CHORK
          Shut up! Just shut up!
               (to himself)
          I work with such dimwits, I swear!
          Utter dimwits!
               (to Gang Guy #2)
          Gimme that!

Chork takes the gun from Gang Guy #2.

                    CHORK
          I'll do it myself.

Sensei Yumi comes on the scene carrying his staff.

                    SENSEI YUMI
          What going on here?

                    CHORK
          Go away, old man! This doesn't
          concern you.

                    SENSEI YUMI
               (irritated)
          What say to me?

                    CHORK
               (to Gang Guy #2)
          Get rid of that prune, will you?

                    GANG GUY #2
          My pleasure.

Gang Guy #2 goes to beat up Yumi. Yumi uses his staff, and within
seconds he's out cold.

                    SENSEI YUMI
          Leave now! Me not say again.

                    GANG GUY #3
               (to Chork all cocky)
          Let me handle this.

Gang Guy #3 cracks his fingers and neck. He picks up a rusted pipe
laying on the side and goes in all big and bad, showing off his
martial art skills.

                                                      (CONTINUED)

                         SENSEI YUMI
                      (to Gang Guy #3)
                  Very wise man said, "No count
                  chickens before hatched."

Gang Guy #3 begins to laugh. The other join in. #3 goes in for the
kill, but fails miserably also. Panic falls on them.

                         SENSEI YUMI
                      (to Gang Guy #3)
                  Me guess, wise man right.

                         CHORK
                  Who are you, old man?

                         SENSEI YUMI
                      (to Chork)
                  Me be nice and give you chance.
                  Leave or I give you something to
                  talk to your mama about.

                         CHORK
                      (to #4 and #5)
                  DON'T STAND THERE, YOU FOOLS. GET HIM!!!

Gang Guy #4 and GANG GUY #5 go to take him down. Again, Yumi takes
both of them down in seconds. Chork signals GANG GUY #6. #6 does a
few scary looking martial arts moves. Yumi gets into fighting
position and gives #6 the "come get me" signal. Immediately, #6
dashes off like a total coward.

                         SENSEI YUMI
                  Is down to you and me.

                         CHORK
                  Who are you, old man? Who are you!?

                         SENSEI YUMI
                  Who me, not matter.

Yumi picks up two golf ball size rocks.

                         CHORK
                  You messed with the wrong guy, old
                  man. Do you "even" know who I am?

Chork points the gun at him and pulls the trigger, but
nothing. He pulls it again, still nothing.

                         SENSEI YUMI
                  You mess with wrong guy too,>>>

***************************SLOW MOTION***************************

Yumi throws both rocks into the air and hits them with the staff.
Both rocks brush against Chork's left cheek, breaking the skin.

***************************BACK TO NORMAL***************************

                         SENSEI YUMI
                  >>>cause no care who are... "even."

                                                          (CONTINUED)

Chork wipes the blood off his cheek.

> CHORK
> You may have won this round, old man,
> but this fight is far from over.

Chork looks around for a moment and sees his beaten-up gang.

> CHORK
> I will be back. Be certain of it!

Tore up good by Bark, Chork limp-walks to his car, along with the others who are still conscious.

150   **INT. YUMI'S PLACE/KITCHEN - DAY**

Jake(carrying BARK) and Sensei Yumi enter in a rush.

> SENSEI YUMI
> On table.

Jake places Bark on the table.

> JAKE
> Do you think he'll live?

Yumi checks out Bark's leg.

> SENSEI YUMI
> Bullet go through. No broken bones.

> JAKE
> That's good, right?

> SENSEI YUMI
> Yes. Very good. Go there, first
> drawer, bring red box quickly.

Jake goes over there and finds it.

> JAKE
> This one?

> SENSEI YUMI
> Yes. Bring it!

Jake gives it to him. Yumi mixes his oriental concoction.

> JAKE
> What is it?

> SENSEI YUMI
> Japanese secret medicine given to
> me from Great Grandfather.

> JAKE
> Ohhhhhhhhhh...

Moment of silence as Yumi tends to Bark's leg.

(CONTINUED)

                              SENSEI YUMI
                    Why Japanese Mafia after you?

                              JAKE
                    Is that who that was?

                              SENSEI YUMI
                    Why after you?

          Yumi applies the medicine to the leg. Bark whines a bit.

                              SENSEI YUMI
                    Good doggy.

                              JAKE
                    His name is Bark.

                              SENSEI YUMI
                    Why after you, my son?

                              JAKE
                    I don't know why they're after me.

                              SENSEI YUMI
                    How you not know? They know.

                              JAKE
                    I hit a tree with my car and woke
                    up with amnesia.

                              SENSEI YUMI
                    You have name?

                              JAKE
                    Isaac- Oh wow!

          Jake swallows with grief.

                              JAKE
                    It's Jake. Jake Daniels.

                              SENSEI YUMI
                    Me hear that name before. Come to think,
                    Me see face before too. You not Jake
                    "The Ice" Daniels, the karate idiot?

                              JAKE
                    No, I don't think so.

                              SENSEI YUMI
                         (suspiciously)
                    Very much, look as him.

          Sensei Yumi finishes bandaging Bark.

                              SENSEI YUMI
                    I, Sensei Yumi. Sensei, if you like.

                              JAKE
                    Sure.

Sensei Yumi pulls out an onion, bacon, and bread, and slices
and dices them, like a professional chef.

> JAKE
> That smells pretty good. What
> you making?

> SENSEI YUMI
> Bread, Bacon, Onion, all cut up.

> JAKE
> Ohhhh...

> SENSEI YUMI
> Put in mouth and chew. No swallow.

Jake takes them and chews it.

> JAKE
> (semi-muffled)
> What's this for?

> SENSEI YUMI
> No talk. Just chew.

Yumi pulls out some medical gauze pads.

> SENSEI YUMI
> Good! Put chew on pad.

Jake does.

> JAKE
> What are you gonna do with it?

> SENSEI YUMI
> Put on wound.

> JAKE
> Whaaaaaaaaat!?

> SENSEI YUMI
> What "what?" Me put chew on wound,
> that what.

Sensei Yumi goes to put it on his arm.

> JAKE
> (with rejection)
> Ohhhh, hold on for just a second,
> Sensei! You sure that's necessary?

> SENSEI YUMI
> Arm bruised badly. Very necessary.

> JAKE
> Can't you just give me your
> grandfather's secret medicine.

> SENSEI YUMI
> You want animal medicine!?

                    JAKE
          This is animal medicine.

                    SENSEI YUMI
          Not animal medicine! People medicine.

                    JAKE
          So what happens if you just give me
          what you gave Bark?

                    SENSEI YUMI
          Me not know. Never try. You want to
          be animal, and try?

Jake ponders for a moment and gives a sigh of defeat.

151   **INT. YUMI'S PLACE/DOJO - DAY**

Sensei Yumi and Jake(arm bandaged) enter a dark room.

                    JAKE
          This has got to be one of the
          grossest things I have ever done.
          I'm not sure, but it has to be.

                    SENSEI YUMI
          Not gross, my son. Medicine
          very-very good.
                    (to himself)
          Now where those lights?

The lights come on. It's a huge room full of martial arts equipment.
Championship flags are hanging from the ceiling, hanging on the
walls, etc... Jake looks around in total awe.

                    JAKE
          Wow! Would you look at this place!

                    SENSEI YUMI
          I teach martial arts 40+ years,
          before I retire.

Jake takes the floor and does some great moves.

                    SENSEI YUMI
          Have good form, my son, but balance
          need much work.

                    JAKE
          Just look at all those trophies! I'm
          terribly impressed, Sensei.

                    SENSEI YUMI
          Medals and trophies, yes. National
          championship, no.

                    JAKE
          You've never won a national
          championship and you've been doing
          this for more than 40 years?

(CONTINUED)

>   SENSEI YUMI
>   In youth, Me win many national
>   championships. But shamefully, not
>   as teacher. Many fighters come and
>   go, but none worthy to wear
>   Warrior's Uniform.

>   JAKE
>   Warrior's Uniform?

>   SENSEI YUMI
>   Come, I show.

152   **INT. YUMI'S PLACE/MUSEUM ROOM - DAY**

Sensei Yumi opens the door and turns on the lights. Jake follows him.
Yumi approaches the stand with the covered-up monument. He slides off
the black cloth with one slow pull.

>   SENSEI YUMI
>   Here she is. Warrior's Uniform.

An awesome looking martial arts uniform, encased in a glass case, is
revealed. JAKE is totally awed by its magnificence.

>   JAKE
>   It's a work of art, Sensei.

>   SENSEI YUMI
>   Wife make for me. Is uniform me
>   wear in competitions, many-many
>   years ago, but no find fighter
>   worthy to wear it.

>   JAKE
>   What kind of training does one
>   go through to become worthy?

>   SENSEI YUMI
>   No training, my son.

>   JAKE
>   No training! Really!?

>   SENSEI YUMI
>   No training. Come, I show something.

Yumi plugs a VHS tape in a VCR. We see a montage on TV of the best
fighters that he has trained.

>   JAKE
>   You trained them?

>   SENSEI YUMI
>   Yes.

>   JAKE
>   They are good.

                                                      (CONTINUED)

                         SENSEI YUMI
               This one best student. We hopeful
               to go Nationals with him.

                         JAKE
               And what happened?

Suddenly, an opposing fighter breaks the student's arm.

                         JAKE
               Ouch!

                         SENSEI YUMI
               He never fight again.

Sensei Yumi takes out the tape and picks up another.

                         SENSEI YUMI
               This one take much time to make,
               so pay attention.

He slides in the tape. It's a montage video of Jake fighting
in tournaments.

                         JAKE
                    (curious)
               He kinda looks like me. Is it me?

Jake watches the fight and after a moment it begins to get brutal
and more brutal.

                         JAKE
                    (with regret)
               That is me.

Jake can't take it anymore.

                         JAKE
               Turn it off.

                         SENSEI YUMI
               Pay attention. Last part coming.

                         JAKE
               No, I don't want to see anymore.

                         SENSEI YUMI
               Almost there.

Suddenly, Jake breaks Bruce's leg so badly, it bends back like
rubber. Grieved by what he saw, Jake walks away toward the corner
of the room with grief and regret.

                         JAKE
               That's not me.

                         SESNEI YUMI
               Is you, my son.

Jake turns to Yumi.

                         JAKE
             No! That is someone that looks like me,
             but that is not who I am (sigh) in here.

Jake points to his heart.

                         SENSEI YUMI
             If not you, then who? Who is Jake Daniels?

Jake takes a deep sigh.

                         JAKE
             I don't know. (sigh)

Yumi turns off the TV. He walks towards the Warrior's Uniform and
stares at it for a moment, then looks over at Jake.

                         SENSEI YUMI
             You believe in fate, my son?

                         JAKE
             No.

                         SENSEI YUMI
             Why not?

                         JAKE
             Because I don't like the idea of
             not being in control of my own life.

                         SENSEI YUMI
             Me believe, and maybe God bring you
             here for purpose?

                         JAKE
             Or it could be by chance.

                         SENSEI YUMI
             No! Not chance, my son. You here to
             give me and give you, second chance.
             You not remember yourself, but everyone
             out there remember. Guess how got
             name, "The Ice" Daniels.

Jake ponders on Yumi's comments for a long while. Jake walks over to
the uniform and stares at it.

                         JAKE
             When do the competitions start?

                         SENSEI YUMI
             Started already. We start with last
             place, train hard, fight smart, and
             maybe make it to State.

                         JAKE
             Last place, huh? Do you think we have a chance?

                  SENSEI YUMI
         Chance very little, but we not fight
         for winning. We fight for honor.
         Winning will come on own.

Moment of silence.

                  JAKE
         So what second chance is it for you?

Sensei Yumi gazes at the uniform for a moment.

                  SENSEI YUMI
         Maybe last chance to keep promise
         to very faithful friend.

Jake ponders deeply, then stares back at the uniform.

                  JAKE
         Okay. I'll do it, but what will I
         do about those mafia guys? They'll
         be back, you know they will.

153   **EXT. NIGHT CLUB - NIGHT**

A taxicab pulls in front of the club. Sensei Yumi and Jake
get out. A long line of people are lined up at the door,
which is guarded by Brute #3 and BRUTE #4. Sensei Yumi and
Jake walk up to the front entrance.

                  BRUTE #3
         Sorry, there's an age limit.

                  SENSEI YUMI
         Need to speak to boss.

                  BRUTE #3
         Do you have an appointment?

                  SENSEI YUMI
         No.

                  BRUTE #4
         Then scram.

                  SENSEI YUMI
         Take me to boss or regret it.

Brute #4 gazes over at Brute #3 and they both laugh.

                  BRUTE #3
           (to Brute #4)
         Will you listen to this old fart?
         "Take me to boss." Who does he
         think he is?

Sensei Yumi glances over at Jake.

154   **INT. NIGHT CLUB/DANCE FLOOR - NIGHT**

A rush of people enter the club. BRUTE #5 calls on the radio.

                    BRUTE #5
               (on radio)
          Yo, Skull! What's with the rush
          of people?... Skull!

155   **EXT. NIGHT CLUB - NIGHT**

We see Brute #3 and #4 lay on the floor motionless.

                    BRUTE #5(V.O.)
               (from radio)
          Skull! Answer, man!

The radio lays on the ground beside them.

156   **INT. NIGHT CLUB/DANCE FLOOR - NIGHT**

Sensei Yumi looks around and sees Brute #1 and Brute #2 guarding the
basement door.

                    SENSEI YUMI
          Is this way.

Sensei Yumi approaches them.

                    SENSEI YUMI
          Take me to boss.

Both brutes look at each other.

                    BRUTE #1
          What the--

Yumi leaves them on the floor motionless.

                    SENSEI YUMI
               (to Brutes)
          Need to learn manners.
               (to Jake)
          Come.

157   **INT. NIGHT CLUB STAIRS ---> BASEMENT - NIGHT**

Sensei Yumi and Jake walk down the stairs, past the martial arts
ring, and toward Boss's office.

158   **INT. NIGHT CLUB/BASEMENT/BOSS' OFFICE - NIGHT**

Stacks of counted cash sit on top of the desk, as Boss wraps each
stack with a rubber band and places it in a pile. A white pimp cane
leans against the edge of the table. Sensei Yumi bursts in the office
and quickly approaches him.

                                        (CONTINUED)

                              SENSEI YUMI
                    You the stinking weasel behind this?

Jake stands a few steps behind Yumi.

                              BOSS
                    Who are you, and how did you get
                    past my guards!?

                              SENSEI YUMI
                    Me say, leave Jake Daniels in peace.

Boss stands up in anger.

                              BOSS
                         (with anger)
                    WHO ARE YOU AND HOW DID YOU GET
                    PAST MY GUARDS!? ANSWER ME!!!

                              SENSEI YUMI
                    Ask them yourself when they wake.
                    Leave Jake in peace.

                              BOSS
                    What are you? His grandpa?

                              SENSEI YUMI
                    Jake my friend.

                              BOSS
                    Well, I'm afraid I can't do that, my
                    international mysterious colleague.
                    He owes us money and we'll collect it
                    with his life, if we must.

Chork, with his BRUTES, burst into the office, guns drawn. Instantly,
Yumi takes the ashtray off the table and throws it at one of the
aquariums, shattering it to pieces. The water instantly takes down
Chork and all his Brutes. The piranhas immediately begin to chomp
on them. They scream and yell as they shoot all the piranhas dead.

                              CHORK
                    That's him. That's the guy I told
                    you about.

Boss sneakingly tries to pull the desk drawer open. Yumi quickly
grabs the white pimp cane leaning against the desk, smashes Boss'
hand, and quickly jams it in his throat.

                              BOSS
                    Easy now.

                              SENSEI YUMI
                    Tell them to throw weapons in other
                    aquarium. DO IT!!!

                              BOSS
                         (calm)
                    Why don't you lay down the cane
                    and we'll talk to each other like
                    civilized people?

                                                          (CONTINUED)

> SENSEI YUMI
> Only civilized thing you get
> from me is early retirement.

> BOSS
> You're bluffing.

> SENSEI YUMI
> Sure you play poker face with me?

> BOSS
> Yeah, let's play.

Yumi adds more pressure, as they stare into each other's eyes.

> BOSS
> What are you waiting for? Do it!

> CHORK
> Boss!

Boss signals Chork to stand down.

> BOSS
> Do it! I dare you.

With one hard sweep, Yumi uses the cane to knock down everything off
the desk, quickly returning it to Boss' neck.

> SENSEI YUMI
> (in Japanese)
> I am an old man and have nothing to
> lose. I'll give you this one last
> chance. If I were you, I'd take it.

Yumi presses harder. Beads of sweat flows down Boss' face.

> BOSS
> (choking voice)
> DO WHAT HE SAYS!

> CHORK
> (with hesitation)
> But boss!

> BOSS
> (choking voice)
> GRANDPA'S CRAZY! DO IT NOW!

They all throw their guns in the other aquarium. Sensei Yumi puts
down the cane. Boss coughs for a moment.

> SENSEI YUMI
> Tell me how much he owe? Me pay.

Boss tidies up his clothes.

> BOSS
> What, are you guys like best pals,
> or something?

(CONTINUED)

                         SENSEI YUMI
                Not your business. Me pay, you
                leave Jake alone. Have deal?

Boss looks over at Jake.

                         BOSS
                Sure, why not. Pay us 100K, and
                he's free as a bird.

Yumi looks over at Jake. Jake swallows in fear.

                         SENSEI YUMI
                That lot of money.

                         BOSS
                Well, if money grew on trees, Jake
                would have paid us by now.
                         (to Jake)
                Isn't that right, Jake?

Moment of silence.

                         SENSEI YUMI
                How 'bout me make new deal? Me fight
                back there till all debt paid. Deal?

                         BOSS
                And why should I agree to such terms?

                         SENSEI YUMI
                You make much money with fighting.
                This me know. Me make you much money.

Boss looks over at Chork. Chork shrugs his shoulder.

                         BOSS
                When is the last time you've been
                in a fight, old man?

                         SENSEI YUMI
                1 minutes ago.

Boss realizes Yumi's got a point.

                         BOSS
                         (humbled)
                Touché...

159   **INT. NIGHT CLUB/BASEMENT - NIGHT**

We see the fighting ring with CLUB ANNOUNCER in the center.

                         CLUB ANNOUNCER
                Place your bets, place your bets.

CHORK'S POSITION:

Chork sits in the VIP section. Boss joins him.

                                                      (CONTINUED)

                              BOSS
                    This is gonna be good.

                              CHORK
                    I thought he only owed 50K.

                              BOSS
                    50K, 100K, What's the difference? If what
                    you said is true, they don't know, right?
                    Besides, someone's gotta pay for all that
                    water damage, and it's not gonna be me.

CORNER RING:

Yumi finishes wrapping his karate bandage. Jake's beside him.

                              JAKE
                    Don't do this, Sensei. It's suicide!

Yumi tests his wrap by fisting his palms.

                              CLUB ANNOUNCER(O.S.)
                    And his opponent, Grandpa Yumi.

                              SENSEI YUMI
                         (irritated)
                    Me show them Grandpa.

                              JAKE
                    Please, don't do it! I beg you.

                              SENSEI YUMI
                    Don't worry, my son. It be okay.

Sensei Yumi climbs into the ring.

CENTER RING:

Yumi and KOLE, a white man in his 30's, line up to fight.

                              CLUB REFEREE
                    Ready... FIGHT!

Kole dances the ring all big and bad; just pushing Yumi's buttons.

                              KOLE
                    Which nursing home did you crawl out of?

Kole does some fast, show-off, moves.

                              KOLE
                    Wet your diapers, did we?

                              SENSEI YUMI
                    Never hear that before.

                              KOLE
                    C'mon, Gramps, show me what you
                    got! Show me what you got!

                                                          (CONTINUED)

Yumi takes him down in one quick move.

>   CLUB ANNOUNCER
>   (overhead speakers)
>   And our winner is Grandpa Yumi.

>   SENSEI YUMI
>   (to Club Announcer)
>   Sensei, not Grandpa.

>   CLUB ANNOUNCER
>   You're on my turf now.

VIP SECTION:

With a big smile, Boss' takes a puff of his cigar and blows the smoke
in Chork's face.

>   BOSS
>   I think we got ourselves a winner.

Chork coughs.

160   **EXT. NIGHT CLUB/BACK ALLEY - NIGHT**

Jake and Sensei Yumi, exit the club through the back, followed
by Boss and Chork.

>   BOSS
>   (to Sensei Yumi)
>   Here is the fight schedule.

Boss hands the schedule to both Jake and Yumi. Yumi looks it over and
hands it back to Boss.

>   SENSEI YUMI
>   Have dates in mind. No need paper.

>   BOSS   .
>   Okay, have it your way.

Boss crumples the paper in a ball and shoots it in a nearby dumpster.

>   BOSS
>   That's what I call, "Swoosh!"

Yumi takes Jake's paper and crumples it in a ball. He throws it on
the opposite wall of the club, bounces off that wall, bounces off the
club wall, hits the opened lid of the dumpster and slides right in.

>   CHORK
>   (to Boss)
>   And what you call that, "Hole in one?"

>   BOSS
>   You always have something smart
>   to say, don't you?

They make their way inside the club.

161   **EXT. YUMI'S PLACE - NIGHT**

A taxicab pulls in front of Yumi's place. Sensei Yumi, followed by
Jake, exit the cab. They chat as they make their way to the entrance.

> JAKE
> But I already have an apartment,
> Sensei. It's really nice too.

> SENSEI YUMI
> Me not lie to you, my son. First 3
> weeks training very hard. Training
> start early>>>

The taxicab pulls away in the background.

> SENSEI YUMI
> >>>morning and end late night. You be
> very tired to come and go to apartment.
> Me say, after 3 weeks, then go apartment.

> JAKE
> Okay, I guess I can do that.

> SENSEI YUMI
> Very good.

162   **INT. YUMI'S PLACE/FRONT ENTRANCE - NIGHT**

Sensei Yumi and Jake enter. Bark happily greets them.

> JAKE
> (with excitement)
> Bark! You're alright!

He hugs Bark.

> JAKE
> I'm so happy you're well.
> (to Sensei Yumi)
> The medicine you gave him really
> worked, Sensei! What's in that stuff?

> SENSEI YUMI
> Me not know. Medicine is secret.

Bark starts licking Jake's face.

> JAKE
> Blahhhh! The licking has got to go, Bark.

> SENSEI YUMI
> Why you name doggy, Bark? Is like
> naming doggy, Doggy.

> JAKE
> He was given to me with the name.

> SENSEI YUMI
> Not very creative, if ask me. Come I
> introduce you to first training.

163   **INT. YUMI'S PLACE/KITCHEN - NIGHT**

Jake and Sensei Yumi sit at the kitchen table. Yumi mixes a deck of poker cards like a professional casino dealer.

> JAKE
> Were you a casino dealer?

> SENSEI YUMI
> Not matter. Just pay attention.

He sets 5 cards down(face up), scattered all over the table.

> SENSEI YUMI
> Take mental picture of where cards on
> table. When ready, put blindfold and
> put finger on every card. Say what card
> is. Here, I show.

Yumi closes his eyes and puts his finger on every card and verbally tells Jake the card.

> JAKE
> That's amazing, Sensei! How did you
> do that?

> SENSEI YUMI
> Is called training. Now you try.

> JAKE
> You sure I can do this? I don't
> have a photographic memory, at
> least I don't think I do.

> SENSEI YUMI
> Everyone have little photographic
> memory. Some more, some less, but
> need to be trained.

Jake begins to study the cards for a moment. He swings the blindfold over his eyes and tries it, but fails miserably.

> JAKE
> How did I do?

> SENSEI YUMI
> I think Bark can do better.
>   (to Bark)
> What you think, Bark?

Dog barks.

> SENSEI YUMI
> Me like your doggy. He smart
> like me.

> JAKE
> Okay, this is all great, but how
> will this help me win competitions?

(CONTINUED)

                              SENSEI YUMI
                    Mind, eyes, ears; most important asset
                    have as fighter. Take mental picture
                    of target, STRIKE with eyes closed.

Yumi does a karate chop.

                              JAKE
                    Fight with my eyes closed!?

                              SENSEI YUMI
                    No-no, my son. Strike with eyes
                    closed. Like this.

Yumi closes his eyes.

                              SENSEI YUMI
                    Mental picture of target, and>>>

He launches a karate chop to Jake's face.

                              SENSEI YUMI
                    >>>STRIKE! Eyes closed.

Jake flinches, quickly backing away.

                              JAKE
                    Wow, that was fast! So where do the
                    ears fall in?

                              SENSEI YUMI
                    Ears only used to adjust target before
                    strike. If target move, listen and adjust.
                    Fighting always mind first, body second.
                    You not know now, but will later.

                              JAKE
                    Okay, hit me.

Yumi quickly gives Jake a light smack across the face.

                              JAKE
                    I didn't mean for real.

                              SENSEI YUMI
                    Me know! Testing reaction and reaction
                    suck, but we work on that too.

                              JAKE
                    Do it again. I'm sure I can do better.

                              SENSEI YUMI
                    You practice on own, but practice much.
                    Very-very important, okay? Come, I show
                    you sleeping room.

164   **INT. YUMI'S PLACE/JAKE'S ROOM - NIGHT**

Jake and Sensei Yumi enter a room with only a bed against the corner.
Bark limps along.

> SENSEI YUMI
> Not much, I know, but will do.

> JAKE
> At least it's not the barn.

> SENSEI YUMI
> Barn?

> JAKE
> Nothing.

> SENSEI YUMI
> Breakfast 4AM sharp. 4:30 we train.

> JAKE
> Got it. Where's my alarm clock?

> SENSEI YUMI
> Me alarm clock. Get good rest, my
> son. You will need it.

Sensei Yumi leaves, closing the door and lights after him. Street
lights shine through the window.

> JAKE
> I'm so exhausted, Bark.

Jake crashes on the bed.

> JAKE
> I'm so happy that you're well...(sigh).

Jake immediately falls asleep. We slowly slide into his face.

DOOR: KNOCK-KNOCK-KNOCK!!!

> SENSEI YUMI
> It's 4am my son. Get up!

> JAKE
> What!?

> SENSEI YUMI
> Come, Come! Breakfast on the table.

VOCAL FAITH SONG BEGINS...

165   **TRAINING AND COMPETITION MONTAGE**

We see a montage of Sensei Yumi training Jake, showing him where and
how to hit, and so on... Getting better and better.

Montage continues with Jake fighting in the competitions, slowly
making his way up the championship ladder.

(CONTINUED)

Jake also practices the card training, along with Yumi having him do all sorts of blindfolded training exercises.

Jake tries to hit a training dummy, blindfolded.

> SENSEI YUMI
> Take picture. Strike!

Jake peeks through the blindfold and strikes.

> SENSEI YUMI
> You hit with anger, my son.

> JAKE
> Because I can't do it.

> SENSEI YUMI
> Anger keeps mind cluttered and
> unfocused. Fight with clear mind.

This montage is intercut with Yumi fighting at the night club winning fight after fight. We see the Boss is super pleased.

VOCAL FAITH SONG ENDS.

166   **INT. COMPETITION FLOOR - NIGHT**

Commentator Ty and Commentator Dave comment after the match.

> COMMENTATOR TY
> (to TV Audience)
> What an amazing season. Jake "The Ice"
> Daniels is back on the Richter Scale,
> folks. Who woulda thought!

> COMMENTATOR DAVE
> (to TV Audience)
> Daniels acquired the help of long retired
> martial arts instructor, Sensei Yumi, who,
> in his own right, has taken home many national
> titles, but never a national title as a martial
> arts instructor. Will the streak of bad luck
> continue to haunt him, or will his luck change
> with Jake "The Ice" Daniels on his side?

> COMMENTATOR TY
> (to TV audience)
> Only the top 3 fighters from each state will
> be allowed to compete in the Nationals held
> in Detroit. Will Jake Daniels be among them?
> We shall see soon enough.

> COMMENTATOR DAVE
> (to TV audience)
> We are Pennsylvania's exclusive Martial
> Arts Commentators, Dave Karnie.

> COMMENTATOR TY
> (to TV audience)
> And Ty Gordon. See you in Philly for
> the state finals. Have a blessed night.

The camera pulls back as they chit-chat between themselves.

167   EXT. MT. JOY - DAY

Timmy, Amish Teen #1, and Amish Teen #2 stand in a circle.

          AMISH TEEN #2
    We have been doing this for weeks.
    We will get caught, one day.

          TIMMY
    There is a first for everything, my
    brother. You both ready?

They all look at each other.

          AMISH TEEN #1   AMISH TEEN #2
Yes.   Yes.

          TIMMY
    Go!

They split into 3 directions. Amish Teen #1 and #2 meet up near the
"Country Gazette" newspaper stand and pretend they just bumped into
each other. As they converse, Timmy sneaks behind them. We hear
change dropping into the paper stand and the door being pulled open.

          TIMMY
    I got it!

They take off in a hurry, but within seconds Timmy smacks directly
into Abe, knocking him down to the ground.

          TIMMY
    I am terribly sorry, Brother Abe.
    I did not see you.

As Timmy helps Abe up, Abe spots the newspaper on the ground and
picks it up.

          AMISH TEEN #1
    Time to go.

          AMISH TEEN #2
    Wait for me!

Amish Teen #1 and #2 leave.

          TIMMY
    I certainly can explain that. Uhhhh...

Abe stares at the paper and is awed by what he sees.

NEWSPAPER: *"THE ICE" MAKES IT TO FINALS BY A SLITHER."*

          ABE
    (to Timmy)
    This is Brother Isaac on the front.

168   **INT. YUMI'S PLACE/DOJO - DAY**

Jake goes through the same obstacle course Sensei Yumi has done at
the beginning of the movie, performing the same acrobatic moves.
BARK watches from the sidelines.

> JAKE
> Did you put all your students
> through this kind of torture?

> SENSEI YUMI
> Only ones I like.

> JAKE
> Then I guess you must really love
> me, huh?

Jake jumps off the last equipment and lands perfectly.

> SENSEI YUMI
> Good job, my son. Now again.
> This time, wear this.

Yumi holds out the blindfold.

> JAKE
> You're kidding, right? You don't mean—

> SENSEI YUMI
> You practice cards, yes?

> JAKE
> (hesitantly)
> Uhhhhhhh, Yeah sure.

> SENSEI YUMI
> Good. Now put what learn to practice.

Jake hesitantly takes the blindfold and gets into position.

> JAKE
> I don't know, Sensei. I don't feel
> right about this.

> SENSEI YUMI
> Just try. If get hurt, say "ouch."

He stares at the course for a tad and puts on the blindfold.

> JAKE
> Okay, here goes nothing.

Jake takes a few deep breaths. He peaks again.

> SENSEI YUMI
> No fear, my son.

> JAKE
> (softly to himself)
> No fear. No fear!

(CONTINUED)

He starts, instantly crashing on the first obstacle.

                    JAKE
          OUUUUUUUUUUUUUUUUUUCH!

SENSEI YUMI'S POSITION:

Sensei Yumi laughs his heart out.

                    SENSEI YUMI
          Go kiss his boo-boo, Bark!

Bark takes off quickly.

                    JAKE(O.S.)
          BAAAAAAAAAAAAAAAAAAARK!!!

Sensei Yumi laughs even harder.

169   **INT. JAPANESE RESTAURANT/FRONT ENTRANCE - NIGHT**

Jake and Sensei Yumi enter a very nice Japanese Restaurant.

                    SENSEI YUMI
          This favorite place in town.

They approach JAPANESE HOSTESS, a female in her 40's.

                    JAPANESE HOSTESS
               (in Japanese)
          Welcome back, Sensei. Same place?

                    SENSEI YUMI
               (in Japanese)
          Yes, thank you.

She leaves.

                    JAKE
          It's a very nice, Sensei.
          What's the occasion?

                    SENSEI YUMI
          You pass most hard part of training
          in record time.

                    JAKE
          Oh yeah!? What was the record before?

                    SENSEI YUMI
          6 months.

                    JAKE
          Really!? How is that possible?

                    SENSEI YUMI
          I do cram in 3 weeks. I no have
          choice. Sorry.

                                              (CONTINUED)

                        JAKE
              That explains why my whole body
              aches like crazy.

Jake holds and moves his shoulder in a circular motion.

                        SENSEI YUMI
              Ahhhhhh! But good pain make you good
              strong. And good strong make you good.

                        JAKE
              I certainly hope so.

Japanese Hostess comes back.

                        JAPANESE HOSTESS
                   (in Japanese)
              Right this way.

170   **INT. JAPANESE RESTAURANT/DINING CUBICLE - NIGHT**

Jake and Sensei Yumi sit on the floor across from each other. SUSHI
CHEF, a Japanese man in his 60's, brings a boat of sushi and sets
it on the table.

                        SUSHI CHEF
                   (in Japanese)
              Enjoy.

                        SENSEI YUMI
                   (in Japanese)
              Thank you.

Jake takes a sushi off the boat, smells it, and pops it in.

                        JAKE
                   (with disgust)
              How can you eat this, Sensei?

                        SENSEI YUMI
              No good, my son. No take and scarf
              down like slob. Sushi to be eaten
              proper way. Here, I show.

Yumi makes his own concoction dip, takes a piece of sushi with his
chopsticks, dips it in, and gives it to him.

                        SENSEI YUMI
              Try.

Jake grabs his chop sticks, but can't figure it out. He takes the
sushi with his fingers and pops it in his mouth.

                        JAKE
              Hey! That's not bad. Not bad at all.

                        SENSEI YUMI
              This one here>>>

Yumi points to a different sushi roll from the boat.

                                                        (CONTINUED)

                              SENSEI YUMI
                    >>>need different mix.

Yumi mixes a new dip, takes the sushi roll with his chopsticks and
dips it into new mix, and eats it.

                              SENSEI YUMI
                         (to himself)
                    Hmmmmm... If there food in heaven,
                    me hope it be sushi.
                         (to Jake)
                    You try.

Jake mixes Yumi's recipe.

                              SENSEI YUMI
                    Good-good. Not too much. Not too much.
                    Now mix slowly... There, Is good.

Jake picks up the sushi with his fingers dips it in the
mixture and pops it in.

                              JAKE
                    Wow! It's pretty good, Sensei!

                              SENSEI YUMI
                    Mrs. show me proper way to eat sushi.
                    Before Mrs. Me eat sushi like slob too.
                    Wanna see picture of Mrs.?

                              JAKE
                    Sure.

Yumi pulls a picture from his pocket and gives it to him. It's a
picture of Sensei Yumi and his wife, back when they were much
younger, along with their 9-year-old boy.

                              SENSEI YUMI
                    Her name MiMi. Over 50 years we
                    married.

                              JAKE
                    What happened to her?

                              SENSEI YUMI
                    She die of cancer years ago.

                              JAKE
                    Oh, I'm sorry, Sensei.

                              SENSEI YUMI
                    Me not sorry. She in much better
                    place. No more pain, no more tears.

                              JAKE
                    And how old is your son now?

                              SENSEI YUMI
                    Had son. Pneumonia took life when
                    12 years old.

                                                              (CONTINUED)

Jake swallows with remorse and hands the picture back.

> SENSEI YUMI
> You have friend girl, my son?

> JAKE
> You mean girlfriend?

> SENSEI YUMI
> Friend girl, Girlfriend. Same
> difference.

> JAKE
> Yes, I mean no.

> SENSEI YUMI
> (confused)
> Yes, no? Which is it?

> JAKE
> No.

> SENSEI YUMI
> You say "yes" first time.

> JAKE
> She's this girl I used to know. Not
> that important.

> SENSEI YUMI
> How come me thinks she more than
> just girl you know?

Jake ponders for a moment.

> JAKE
> Her name is Gracie. Gracie Jacobs.

> SENSEI YUMI
> Gracie Jacobs, aye?

> JAKE
> Yeah. She's Amish. She's the one
> that saved me from the car
> accident. Her and her brother.

> SENSEI YUMI
> Amish? Getting interesting.

> JAKE
> It's kind of a long story. I don't
> want to get into it.

> SENSEI YUMI
> She pretty, yes?

Jake blushes for a moment.

(CONTINUED)

                        JAKE
              There's no words to describe her
              beauty, Sensei. I wish I had a
              picture to show you.

                        SENSEI YUMI
              You love girl, yes?

Moment of silence as Jake ponders.

                        JAKE
              Yes. I do love her.

                        SENSEI YUMI
              And she love you?

                        JAKE
              She never told me, but I believe
              she does, or at least did.

Jake gives off an emotional sigh. Moment of silence.

                        JAKE
              What can I say? It just wasn't
              meant to be.

                        SENSEI YUMI
              You no believe in fate, remember?

Jake nods his head.

                        JAKE
              Yeah, you got me.

Moment of silence as Yumi ponders.

                        SENSEI YUMI
              Me heard wise man say, "If love
              something, set it free. If comes
              back to you, it's meant to be."

Jake ponders for a moment.

                        JAKE
              Yeah, I like it. Not sure if it
              applies to me, but I like it.

171   **EXT. JAPANESE RESTAURANT - NIGHT**

Jake and Sensei Yumi exit the restaurant and walk toward the Audi
SUV, which is parked directly in front.

                        JAKE
              Thanks for dinner, and showing me
              the right way to eat sushi.

                        SENSEI YUMI
              Sometimes, good things come in life
              later, me say.

                                                          (CONTINUED)

                         GINA(O.S.)
              Jake?

Jake turns around and gets a hard slap from Gina. She has a trashy
look and feel to her, nothing like before.

                         GINA
              You are such a jerk! You don't text
              me, you don't call me, and leave me
              worried sick!!!

                         JAKE
              I'm sorry, but do I know you!?

She goes for another slap, but Jake grabs her arm.

                         GINA
              HOW DARE YOU!?

                         JAKE
              Do we know each other?

She tries to slap him with her other arm, but Jake grabs it.

                         GINA
              LET GO OF ME, YOU NO-GOOD JERK!
              INSTEAD OF AN APOLOGY, YOU WANNA
              PLAY THESE CHILDISH GAMES?

Sensei Yumi laughs.

                         SENSEI YUMI
              Look like you in big trouble.

                         JAKE
              I could really use your help, Sensei.

Gina stomps on his foot. Jake holds in the pain.

                         JAKE
                    (to Sensei Yumi)
              Like right now would be nice.

                         SENSEI YUMI
              Mother say never get involved
              in family matters, but okay, I
              break rule this time.
                    (to Gina)
              Jake no remember nuttin'. Poof-poof!
              Memory go bye-bye and go koo-koo!

Sensei Yumi circles his finger on his head.

                         JAKE
              You're not helping, Sensei.

                         GINA
                    (to Sensei Yumi)
              Like what, he's got amnesia, or
              something?

                    JAKE
          That's exactly right.

                    GINA
          Oh, well that changes everything,
          doesn't it?

Gina calms down. Jake let's go of her arms, but immediately she
slaps him again.

                    JAKE
          What was that for?

                    GINA
          Force of habit, sorry.

                    SENSEI YUMI
          You old girlfriend?

                    GINA
          That's exactly who I am. I'm his
          girlfriend, Gina. Or should I say,
                    (to Jake)
          ex-girlfriend, Gina. What happened
          to you, Jake? Where have you been
          this whole time?

                    SENSEI YUMI
          Look like you two have catching
          up to do. I go bye-bye.

Sensei Yumi walks away.

                    JAKE
          Hey! Where you going?

                    SENSEI YUMI
          Home.

                    JAKE
          You're gonna walk 2 miles through
          shark infested waters?

                    SENSEI YUMI
          Me eat sharks for breakfast. Don't forget
          we have training tomorrow. 7am sharp.

Sensei Yumi walks away whistling a church song.

172   **INT. 60'S DINER/TABLE - NIGHT**

Jake and Gina sit at a table of a 60's Classic Diner.

                    GINA
          I still can't believe you don't
          remember this place. It was one of
          our favorite places to eat.

                    JAKE
          I wish I could.

                                                    (CONTINUED)

GINA'S CO-WORKER, a black female in her 30's, walks over to them
with two milk shakes and sets them on the table.

                    GINA'S CO-WORKER
          Hey Gina, I've got a doctor's
          appointment tomorrow. You think
          you can cover me for a few hours?

                    GINA
          Yeah, that's fine.

                    GINA'S CO-WORKER
          Thanks. I owe you one.

Gina's co-worker leaves.

                    GINA
          So was that your new karate teacher?

                    JAKE
          I guess you could call him that.

                    GINA
          You think you got a chance? You
          gotta be in last place.

                    JAKE
          Actually, we made it to State.

                    GINA
          Oh wow! That's great, Jake!
          You think you'll go all the way?

                    JAKE
          It would be nice, but it's not
          about winning.

A look of confusion falls on her face.

                    GINA
          Not about winning!? What do you
          mean not about winning? If it's not
          about winning, what's it about?

                    JAKE
          Do you know why they call me Jake
          "The Ice" Daniels?

                    GINA
          I don't know. Cause you're really good.

                    JAKE
          No, it's because I broke peoples arms and
          legs. I fought like a mad man, without,
          heart, without any mercy.

                    GINA
          So what! Bad things happen in this
          sport. If they can't take it, get out!

                                                        (CONTINUED)

                         JAKE
              But I don't want to be remembered that
              way, Gina. It's not who I am anymore.

                         GINA
              So like what? This thing is about
              changing your image? Is that it?

                         JAKE
              A part of it, yes, but it's deeper
              than that.

                         GINA
              How deeper?

Jake takes a deep breath and ponders for a moment.

                         JAKE
              I don't know exactly how to explain
              it, I just know I need to do this.
              If I win, that's great! If I don't,
              I'll be okay with that too.

Moment of silence as Gina ponders.

                         GINA
              I know you lost your memory, and
              all, but it's odd hearing you
              talk like this.

PHONE TEXT RING: CHA-CHING!

Gina looks over her smartphone.

                         GINA
              Oh, I'm so sorry, but I've gotta
              meet someone in 20 minutes. I
              completely forgot about it.

                         JAKE
              Do you need a ride?

                         GINA
              It's only a few blocks to my apartment.

173   **EXT. PITTSBURGH NEIGHBORHOOD - NIGHT**

Jake and Gina walk the sidewalk of a rundown neighborhood.

                         GINA
              And you said to me, "There's
              something wrong with my phone.
              It doesn't have your number in
              it." I fell for you right there.

                         JAKE
              That's what I said, huh?

                         GINA
              Uh-huh, we clicked instantly.

                                                      (CONTINUED)

                    JAKE
          Anything else you could tell me
          about myself?

                    GINA
          Let me think... Oh, that's right!
          Do you know you can paint? You're
          pretty good too.

                    JAKE
          Yes, I saw the paintings.

                    GINA
          You painted a portrait of me too,
          but you never finished it.

                    JAKE
          Oh, I'm sorry.

Moment of silence as they continue walking.

                    GINA
          How's your mother, by the way?

                    JAKE
               (surprised)
          You know my mother?

                    GINA
          Well yeah, of course! I was your
          girlfriend for almost a year, duh!

                    JAKE
          What's her name and where can I
          find her?

                    GINA
          Flora, but everyone calls her, Flo.
          It's the last trailer park on 88
          south, just before you leave the city.

                    JAKE
          What about my father? What's his name?

                    GINA
          You know, you never talked to me
          about him. Do you think you can
          come over and finish it?

                    JAKE
               (confused)
          Finish it?

                    GINA
          You know, the painting?

                    JAKE
          Oh, I don't know, Gina. I'm pretty
          busy with training and the competitions.

                                              (CONTINUED)

                              GINA
                    Okay... But maybe after the
                    competitions?

                              JAKE
                    Yeah, sure. Why not?

They stop walking in front of a rundown apartment building.

                              GINA
                    This is it. I appreciate you walking
                    me home. Would you like to come up?

                              JAKE
                    No, I better be getting back. The
                    training Sensei puts me through is
                    beyond exhausting.

                              GINA
                    Just for a moment. I want to show
                    you that portrait you painted of me.

                              JAKE
                    I don't know. It is—

                              GINA
                         (with twinkle in eye)
                    C'mon Jakey Poo! I really want you
                    to see it.

Moment of silence as Jake ponders insecurely.

174   **INT. APARTMENT BUILDING/GINA'S PLACE - NIGHT**

Gina enters the apartment, followed by Jake.

                              GINA
                    Make yourself at home. I'm gonna
                    freshen up a bit.

                              JAKE
                    Sure.

                              GINA
                    Do you want anything?

She throws him a subtle sexual tease.

                              GINA
                    Anything at all?

                              JAKE
                    I'm good.

She looks around in confusion. She opens the door to the bedroom,
but doesn't go in. She looks back at Jake.

                              GINA
                    You know something, Jake.

                                                            (CONTINUED)

                    JAKE
          Yes.

                    GINA
          You're not at all the same Jake I knew.

                    JAKE
          Is that a compliment?

                    GINA
          I don't know. It just feels weird to
          know somebody and at the same time
          not know them at all.

                    JAKE
          I'm sorry.

                    GINA
          No-no! I'm not blaming you. I'm
          just saying.

Moment of silence.

                    GINA
          I'll be out in a few. There's refreshments
          in the fridge if you want anything.

                    JAKE
          Okay.

Gina enters the bedroom.

DOOR: KNOCK-KNOCK!!!

                    JAKE
               (to Gina)
          Someone's at the door.

                    GINA
               (from inside bedroom)
          Could you get it, please? If it's
          Larry. Just tell him, "The cat is
          doing well."

175   **INT. APARTMENT BUILDING/HALLWAY/GINA'S DOOR - NIGHT**

Wearing a pair of sunglasses, Larry the PACKAGE DELIVERY GUY, a gum
chewing, man in his 30's, with a deep British accent, knocks on the
door. He constantly checks his back while rubbing his nose. Jake
opens the door.

                    PACKAGE DELIVERY GUY
          Who are you?

                    JAKE
          I'm a friend of Gina's.

                    PACKAGE DELIVERY GUY
          Is she home?

                                                        (CONTINUED)

CONTINUED:

153.

                    JAKE
          Yes. Are you Larry?

                    PACKAGE DELIVERY GUY
          Yeah, that's me.

                    JAKE
          She told me to tell you, "The cat
          is doing well."

                    PACKAGE DELIVERY GUY
          Glad to hear it.

He gives Jake a thick yellow package.

                    PACKAGE DELIVERY GUY
                    (hinting)
          You have a melodious night, if you
          know what I mean. (wink-wink)

Larry flips up his collar and walks away suspiciously,
checking his back.

176   **INT. APARTMENT BUILDING/GINA'S PLACE - NIGHT**

Jake curiously checks the package as he walks to the couch.

                    GINA(O.S.)
                    (seductive tone)
          Hello, Jake.

He faces Gina. She's wearing a seductive nightgown and is drop dead
gorgeous. She approaches him with a sexual tease in her walk.

                    GINA
          See anything you like?

He stares at her sexual curving body for a moment. He places the
package on the coffee table and clears his throat.

                    JAKE
          I'm sorry. Did I give you the wrong
          signals?

Confusion forms on her face.

                    GINA
          I was hoping, you know, you'd
          finish the portrait you started.

                    JAKE
          I already said I don't have time, and
          besides, I don't have my painting gear
          with me. Could you go change, please?

                    GINA
                    (insulted)
          Change? It's not the first time
          you've seen me like this, Jake.
          What's the big deal?

(CONTINUED)

                         JAKE
          I'd like it if you'd change, Gina,
          or I'll have to leave.

Gina paces around the room extremely irritated.

                         GINA
                    (to herself)
          Oh wow! I don't believe this. I just
          don't believe it. I've never been
          rejected by anyone before.
                    (to Jake)
          Who is she? Who is this fat cow
          I've been replaced with?

                         JAKE
                    (with firmness)
          Don't call her that! Gracie is the
          nicest, sweetest person I know.

                         GINA
          So you've been cheating on me with
          this Gracie bimbo, is that it?

                         JAKE
          Now wait just one second, Gina! How
          could I be cheating on you when
          this is the first time we've met?

Gina paces around furiously.

                         GINA
                    (to herself)
          I can't believe this. I just can't
          believe it.

                         JAKE
          We may have had something special
          at one time, but that was then, and
          this is now.

                         GINA
          GET OUT! GET OUT OF MY HOUSE, YOU
          DIRTY, LYING CHEAT! GET OUT!!!

Jake stares at her for a mere moment then walks towards the door.
Gina picks up the yellow package off the table>>>

                         GINA
          AND NEVER COME BACK!

>>>and throws it at him, just as Jake closes the door. White powder
explodes everywhere. Complete panic comes over her.

                         GINA
          Oh no!

She frantically goes to the door and tries to pick up the powder,
and stuff it back in the package.

                         GINA
          What have I done? I'm dead! I'm so dead!

177   **EXT. APARTMENT BUILDING - NIGHT**

Jake exits the apartment building.

>   GINA(V.O.)
>   (from inside apartment)
>   THEY'RE GONNA KILL ME! WHAT HAVE I DONE!

He looks up at Gina's apartment window, gives a deep sigh, and
walks away.

178   **INT. YUMI'S PLACE/JAKE'S ROOM - MORNING**

Sunshine travels through the window and beats directly on Jake, who
is still in bed. He awakes and looks around lost.

179   **INT. YUMI'S PLACE/KITCHEN - MORNING**

Bark lays on a dog pillow in the corner of the kitchen. Jake walks
in and looks around.

>   JAKE
>   (to Bark)
>   Where's Sensei?

Bark gets up and walks off.

>   JAKE
>   Where you going?

Bark looks back at him and barks.

180   **INT. YUMI'S PLACE/DOJO - DAY**

Bark walks into the Dojo. Jake follows.

>   JAKE
>   Sensei!... Are you in here?

Suddenly, out of nowhere, a BLACK NINJA attacks Jake, knocking him
down to the ground.

>   JAKE
>   What the!

With one flip, Jake quickly recovers. The ninja gets into fight mode
and gives Jake the "come get me" hand signal.

>   JAKE
>   (confused)
>   Sensei, is that you?

Ninja launches at him. Jake quickly defends himself. The fight goes
back and forth, back and forth in the middle of the obstacle course.
Jake gets knocked down to the floor and the Ninja shoots his foot in
Jake's face, stopping just before contact. The ninja takes off his
mask. It's Yumi.

(CONTINUED)

> SENSEI YUMI
> You fight with reaction, my son.
> Not conviction.

> JAKE
> I knew it was you.

Yumi does a few back flips putting some space between them.

> SENSEI YUMI
> Fight with conviction!

> JAKE
> How?

> SENSEI YUMI
> Remove all fear from mind, and
> fight like you won.

Yumi launches himself at Jake. They go back and forth, Yumi takes Jake down once again, launching his foot in his face.

> SENSEI YUMI
> Fear makes mind unfocused. Remove
> fear from mind.

> JAKE
> I'm not afraid.

> SENSEI YUMI
> Then show me, my son. Show me!

Sensei Yumi does a few back flips and disappears from sight. Jake flips to his feet. He walks around deeply focused, searching for Yumi. He breathes heavily.

> JAKE
> (softly to himself)
> No fear. No fear.

Yumi strikes, but Jake quickly counter-strikes with a good blow to the chest, bringing Yumi down hard.

> JAKE
> Ha! I got you!

Yumi lays on the floor motionless.

> JAKE
> (with concern)
> Sensei?

Jake slowly approaches him.

> JAKE
> Sensei, are you alright?

As soon as Jake is within hitting range, Yumi sweeps Jake's legs taking Jake down to the floor, again Yumi launches his foot in Jake's face, stopping just before contact.

(CONTINUED)

                              JAKE
               That wasn't fair. You fooled me.

                              SENSEI YUMI
               You fool yourself, my son. Opponent most
               vulnerable when guard down. Remember that.
               You no make same mistake, or it cost you.

                              JAKE
               I'll definitely keep that in mind.

Yumi helps Jake up.

                              JAKE
               What's next?

                              SENSEI YUMI
               Training for today, done. Go for jog,
               if you like.
                    (to Bark)
               Doggy! Where you go?

Bark quickly comes to Yumi. Yumi hugs and pets him.

                              SENSEI YUMI
               You good doggy! Extra treat for
               you today.

Bark barks with joy.

181   **EXT. PITTSBURG PARK - DAY**

Jake jogs with Bark at his side. WALKING GIRL, a sweet, innocent
girl, in her 20's, closely resembling Gracie, walks with a Golden
Retriever toward Jake on the same path. Just before they pass each
other, she gives him a nice smile.

                              WALKING GIRL
                    Hi.

                              JAKE
                    Hi.

They pass each other. Jake looks back. After a moment, Jake stops
running and rests on a park bench.

                              JAKE
               We should do this more often.

Bark lifts up his paw. Jake shakes it.

                              JAKE
                    It's a deal!

Moment of silence as Jake pets him. He glances over at Walking Girl
once again, and gives off a grieving sigh.

                              JAKE
                    I miss her, Bark.

Jake sighs again and goes into a deep trance.

182   **INT. JACOBS' BARN/JAKE'S ROOM - NIGHT (DAYDREAM)**

Jake sees Gracie take off her head covering.

*******************************SLOW MOTION*******************************

Long graceful hair flows down to her waist. She turns to him.

*******************************BACK TO NORMAL*******************************

Jake approaches her and gazes into her angelic bright eyes. Jake
slowly goes for her lips.

>   SENSEI YUMI(O.S.)
>   If you love girl,>>>

183   **INT. AMISH COUNTRY/PASSENGER TRAIN - DAY (TRAVELING)**

Jake looks out the train window. Sensei Yumi sits beside him.

>   SENSEI YUMI(O.S.)
>   (in the background)
>   >>>so much, then marry her.

Jake turns toward Yumi.

>   JAKE
>   Did you say something?

>   SENSEI YUMI
>   Me say, if love girl so much, take
>   courage, my son, and marry her.

>   JAKE
>   It doesn't work like that, Sensei.
>   Their ways are complicated.

>   SENSEI YUMI
>   How complicated?

>   JAKE
>   I don't know. Just complicated.

Moment of silence.

>   SENSEI YUMI
>   How much you give to be with girl?

Jake ponders for a moment.

>   JAKE
>   I'd give everything.

>   SENSEI YUMI
>   Then do, my son.

>   JAKE
>   Do what?

(CONTINUED)

                          SENSEI YUMI
                Give everything. What you got to lose?

Jake ponders for a moment.

                          JAKE
                I don't know. She could already be
                married for all I know.

                          SENSEI YUMI
                If she love you as you say,
                I no believe she married.

Jake gives a deeps sigh, then looks out the window.

184   **EXT. PHILADELPHIA HOTEL/ROOM - NIGHT**

Jake and Sensei Yumi enter the hotel room.

                          SENSEI YUMI
                We finally here. Thank you, Lord!

Jake crashes on the bed.

                          SENSEI YUMI
                Hungry? Restaurant downstairs.

                          JAKE
                Too tired to think about food. I'm
                just gonna relax and watch TV.

                          SENSEI YUMI
                Okay. I go eat.

Yumi leaves.

185   **EXT. PHILADELPHIA HOTEL/ROOM - NIGHT (LATER)**

Jake lays on the bed surfing the channels. He flips past>>>

                          KARATE TEACHER(TV)
                But maybe you're already enrolled in
                one of those so called "karate schools."

>>>a karate commercial, but after a tad he returns to it.

                          KARATE TEACHER(TV)
                Aren't you tired of your Sensei always
                telling you what you can and can't do?
                BAMM-BAMM! Brainwashing you with all
                sorts of religious trash, telling you
                to refrain from using your raw emotion
                to fight. BAMM-BAMM! You deserve more!
                You deserve better! I'm here to tell you
                that my teachings are different. Your
                emotions give you power, your emotions
                give you strength. They make
                          (MORE)

                                KARATE TEACHER(TV/cont'd)
                    you who you are, so be who you are. Be the
                    fighter you can be, not the wussy fighter
                    your Sensei forces you to be. We're not
                    ordinary, we're extraordinary. Give yourself
                    the respect you deserve and join our fight.
                    Call the number on your screen and be
                    extraordinary right now. BAMM-BAMM!

An expression of arrogant pride forms on Jake's face.

186   **EXT. PHILADELPHIA STADIUM - DAY**

We see an aerial shot of a huge stadium with Philadelphia in the
background.

                                COMMENTATOR TY(V.O.)
                    We are down to the last state competition
                    of the season. There are well over 100
                    fighters on the roster,>>>

187   **INT. PHILADELPHIA STADIUM/COMMENTATOR'S POSITION - DAY**

                                COMMENTATOR TY
                    >>>each of them trying to chisel their
                    name in the Martial Arts history books.

                                COMMENTATOR DAVE
                    But the real question remains, who will
                    be our 3 fighters to go to Detroit and
                    fight for the National Title, and let's
                    not forget that mind-blowing grand prize?

                                COMMENTATOR TY
                    Only time will tell, Dave. Good luck to
                    all our fighters. May the best man win.

188   **INT. PHILADELPHIA STADIUM/LOCKER ROOM - DAY**

Jake gets dressed for the competition. Sensei Yumi is beside him
with a clipboard in his hand.

                                JAKE
                    I feel good, Sensei. Really good!

                                SENSEI YUMI
                    Feeling good, is good!

                                JAKE
                    I feel like I can take on anything. The
                    whole world. Let me at them. BAMM-BAMM!
                    You want some of this? Come get me!
                    BAMM-BAMM! Take that. BAMM-BAMM!

                                SENSEI YUMI
                            (with concern)
                    What this talk my ears hearing?

                                                        (CONTINUED)

                              JAKE
                    What talk?

                              SENSEI YUMI
                    Too much air in head, talk.

                              JAKE
                    What's wrong with being confident?

                              SENSEI YUMI
                    Not hear confidence. Is prideful heart.

                              JAKE
                    So what's wrong with a little
                    pride. I've earned it, haven't I?

                              SENSEI YUMI
                         (Proverbs 16:18 (NKJV))
                    "*Pride goes before destruction, and
                    a haughty spirit before a fall.*" Is
                    in the Bible!

                              JAKE
                    Oh Sensei, why do you have to be
                    such a spoiler?

                              SENSEI YUMI
                    Spoiler?

                              JAKE
                    Yeah. Why don't you let me do what
                    I want for a change?

          An expression of disappointment forms on Yumi's face.

                              SENSEI YUMI
                    Look like me not needed today, Jake
                    Daniels. Good luck with competition.

          Sensei gives Jake the clipboard and walks away.

                              JAKE
                    Oh c'mon, Sensei. Don't be like
                    that... Sensei! Where you going?
                         (a little louder)
                    C'mon, I was only...

          Sensei exits the room.

189   **SHORT MONTAGE OF JAKE IN COMPETITION - DAY**

          We see a short montage of Jake fighting in the competition, winning
          round after round. He fights with raw emotion, close to his old self
          again. An expression of concern forms on Yumi's face. Yumi looks up
          at God and shakes his head.

190   **INT. PHILADELPHIA STADIUM - DAY**

YUMI'S POSITION:

Sensei Yumi watches from the sidelines. Jake enters.

> JAKE
> I'm such on a roll today, Sensei.
> Nothing can stop me now. Bamm-Bamm!
> Where do we stand?

> SENSEI YUMI
> What you mean, "we?" You on your
> own, remember? Bamm-Bamm!

> JAKE
> You're not sore about what I said in the
> locker room, are you? I did it, Sensei.
> I'm going to Nationals. WOOHOOOOOOOOOOOO!
> C'mon! Celebrate with me!

> SENSEI YUMI
> What celebrate? You not win nothing.

> JAKE
> But I will! You'll see.

> SENSEI YUMI
> How so sure?

> JAKE
> Because I didn't make it this far
> to go home a loser, right?

> SENSEI YUMI
> Head so full of air, not sure if hot
> or cold, but not matter. Let some
> out before head blow up.

> JAKE
> I don't care what you say, Sensei.
> I'm in! I'm going to Nationals.

Jake walks away.

> JAKE
> (as he walks off)
> NATIONALS HERE I COME!

CENTER FLOOR:

Jake and TONY-T, a black man in his 20's, line up to fight.

> PHILADELPHIA REFERREE
> Face each other... Bow... FIGHT!

Jake and Tony-T circle around each other for a moment. Jake goes
for the hits, but Tony outmaneuvers every one of Jake's hits. After
a while Sensei Yumi calls a time out.

(CONTINUED)

CONTINUED: 163.

COMMENTATOR'S POSITION:

> COMMENTATOR TY
> What has happened to Jake Daniels,
> Dave? What happened to him? Doesn't
> he know this is a points competition
> as well? Defense is just as important
> as offense.

> COMMENTATOR DAVE
> Exactly right, Ty! It's as if he threw
> defense completely out the window, but
> the real question here is, "Where is
> Sensei Yumi in all of this?" We didn't
> even see him on the floor today.

YUMI'S POSITION:

Yumi stands on the sidelines holding a bottle of water. Jake
approaches him trying to catch his breath.

> SENSEI YUMI
> For you.

Yumi hands him the bottle. Jake takes it and chugs down half.

> SENSEI YUMI
> Need band-aid too?

> JAKE
> He's kicking my butt, Sensei.

> SENSEI YUMI
> Oh really!? Me not notice.

> JAKE
> What should I do? Tell me!

Jake takes another gulp.

> SENSEI YUMI
> Not sure. Why not ask yourself?

An expression of irritation forms on Jake's face.

> JAKE
> You know, I worked hard to get here.
> I think you owe me a little respect.

> SENSEI YUMI
> You want respect?

> JAKE
> Yeah.

> SENSEI YUMI
> Want it badly?

> JAKE
> Yeah, I do.

(CONTINUED)

Instantly, Yumi smacks him once on his left cheek, very hard.

> SENSEI YUMI
> THEN EARN IT!

COMMENTATOR'S POSITION:

> COMMENTATOR DAVE
> Wou! Did you see that?

> COMMENTATOR TY
> I did! I did!

YUMI'S POSITION:

> SENSEI YUMI
> (aggressive tone)
> WHAT IS HAPPENING TO YOU, MY SON?
> YOU BECOMING OLD SELF AGAIN. CAN
> YOU NOT SEE IT? CAN YOU NOT FEEL
> IT? WAKE UP BEFORE TOO LATE!!!

Yumi's comments begin to take effect in Jake's mind. He lets himself
down to his knees with grief.

> JAKE
> (with remorse)
> Yes. (sigh) You're right, Sensei...
> You're right. My head is full of
> air, just like you said. I don't
> know what came over me. Forgive me,
> Sensei... Forgive me.

> SENSEI YUMI
> Get up, my son. You embarrassing
> yourself, and me too.

Jake gets up. Yumi places his hand on Jake's shoulder.

> SENSEI YUMI
> Is easy to give in to prideful heart.
> Prideful heart come over many former
> students. You not exception.

> JAKE
> Forgive me.

> SENSEI YUMI
> You forgiven, my son.

Yumi gives him a strong manly hug.

> PHILADELPHIA ANNOUNCER
> (overhead speakers)
> Fighters take your places.

Jake wipes his tears.

> JAKE
> What do I do?

>   SENSEI YUMI
>   Win by points not possible. Only
>   option is take him out. If fail,
>   opponent win match and we go home.

Jake bows to Yumi. Yumi returns the bow.

>   JAKE
>   Wish me luck.

>   SENSEI YUMI
>   Do best, and what comes is what comes.

191   **EXT. AMISH COUNTRY ROAD - DUSK**

An Amish carriage approaches a railroad crossing just as the safety
gate swings down.

>   AMISH BUGGY DRIVER
>   Whoaaaaaa!

The carriage stops.

192   **INT. AMISH COUNTRY/PASSENGER TRAIN - DUSK (TRAVELING)**

Jake stares at the Amish carriage as the train passes by. He sighs
with tears in his eyes. Sensei Yumi sits beside him.

>   SENSEI YUMI
>   We won, my son! Why face glum?

Jake gives a deep sigh.

>   JAKE
>   There's this deep feeling of emptiness
>   in my life, Sensei. Like a piece my life
>   is missing and needs to be found.

>   SENSEI YUMI
>   Is about girl?

>   JAKE
>   No, it's not about Gracie. It's deeper.
>   I don't have the words to tell you.

Yumi stares at him with compassion.

>   SENSEI YUMI
>   I pray for you, my son.

>   JAKE
>   Thanks. I need it.

Jake stares out the window and gives a deep sigh.

>   JAKE
>   I messed up back there pretty bad.
>   Even now I feel like such a fool.

                          SENSEI YUMI
              We all make mistake we regret
              later, my son. Learn and move on.

                          JAKE
              Yes, but what happened was not a
              mistake. I literally felt as if I
              was taken over. As if another
              person was controlling my thoughts.

                          SENSEI YUMI
              It was prideful heart, my son.
              Prideful heart from old self.

                          JAKE
              And what if that old prideful heart
              comes back? What do I do then?

                          SENSEI YUMI
              Just say, "no."

                          JAKE
              That's it, just "no!?"

                          SENSEI YUMI
              Just "no."

Moment of silence as Jake ponders.

                          JAKE
              I can do that.
                   (different intonation)
              Yeah, I can do that.

Jake stares out the window for a moment.

                          JAKE
              Could I ask you a personal question,
              Sensei?

                          SENSEI YUMI
              Ask, my son.

                          JAKE
              What made you be a Christian?
              Don't Japanese people have a
              different faith?

                          SENSEI YUMI
              Mrs. born here, in America. She come
              to Japan to be missionary. That how
              we met and how I come to know Jesus.

                          JAKE
              I see, but I still don't understand
              something about you.

                          SENSEI YUMI
              What not understand?

                                              (CONTINUED)

                         JAKE
             How can you love your God after he
             took your son- after he took your
             wife- What is there left to love?

                         SENSEI YUMI
             Oh-ho-ho! You think me not get mad at
             God!? Is that what you think? Oh, I mad
             with God for very-very long time for
             my son. Me even have fight with him.

                         JAKE
             And?

                         SENSEI YUMI
             And what?

                         JAKE
             And why aren't you mad at him now?

                         SENSEI YUMI
             Because he remind me that he too had
             son, and God let son die on cross
             to give me life. That's why me not
             mad no more.

                         JAKE
             Yes, I know the Jesus story, but
             I'm not sure if I can believe it.

                         SENSEI YUM
             Why not believe?

                         JAKE
             It sounds too good to be true. Almost
             like a fairy tale. Just give your life
             to Jesus and "wammo-bammo" all my sins
             are forgiven, and I don't have to do
             anything, but just "have faith?" Who can
             believe that?

                         SENSEI YUMI
             I believe, my son.

                         JAKE
             I'd like to believe too, but how can
             I when I don't even know if it's real?
             I don't want to believe something just
             because someone tells me. I want to
             know it's real for myself.

                         SENSEI YUMI
             I cannot prove what me believe.
             Every person must come to know God
             for himself. Bible says;
                         (Jeremiah 29:13(NKJV))
             "And you will seek Me and find Me, when
             you search for Me with all your heart."
                         (MORE)

                        SENSEI YUMI(cont'd)
                   If want to find God, ask Him to show
                   Himself, and if you ask with true
                   heart, He will show. Me know this
                   because me ask, and He showed.

                        JAKE
                   How, tell me?

Yumi ponders for a tad.

                        SENSEI YUMI
                   When first meet Mrs., all me saw in her
                   is beauty, and boy was she beautiful.
                   Knockout, if you know what me say.
                   Me not care for her religion- just
                   want to date her, but she say to me,
                   "You must first know my God, before
                   can date you." In mind me say, "Me
                   use this to own advantage and charm
                   her to marry me." So she try to show
                   me God, but nothing she say convince me.
                   She finally say, "Me tell you everything,
                   you need to know my God, but now is up
                   to you to know him for yourself." Me love
                   her and wanted to marry her, so me say,
                   "Okay, Me give her God one chance."

                        JAKE
                   And?

                        SENSEI YUMI
                   Me pray to God to show himself to me. That
                   night me have dream that Mrs. and me in
                   heaven, and God marrying us at his altar.
                   It was wonderful dream, and so real too.
                   Next day me see her, she say, "Me have
                   dream with you." Me say, "Me have dream
                   with you too." She say, "Write down dream
                   on paper, and me write down mine." So we
                   both write dreams on paper and give dreams
                   to each other. And we both had same dream.
                   Then me know, like light bulb- "click!">>>

Yumi snaps his fingers.

                        SENSEI YUMI
                   >>>God talk to me through dream. That
                   how me come to believe in God.

                        JAKE
                   That's amazing, Sensei. You think God
                   would talk to me like that?

                        SENSEI YUMI
                   Me say, give him chance, and see.

Jake ponders for a tad and nods.

                                              (CONTINUED)

> SENSEI YUMI
> Sushi for dinner?

> JAKE
> Only if I'm paying.

> SENSEI YUMI
> Wise-man say, "Never pass a
> good offer."... Is deal.

193   **EXT. RITZY HIGH-RISE/FRONT ENTRANCE - NIGHT**

A taxicab pulls in front of Jake's apartment building.

194   **INT. TAXICAB - NIGHT**

Sensei Yumi and Jake are in the back of the cab; bags of Chinese
Takeout in-between them. JAKE exits and chats through the car door.

> SENSEI YUMI
> Sushi getting warm, and warm
> sushi no good. Come back fast.

> JAKE
> In and out. I promise.

Jake leaves. After a tad, Yumi opens a bag and looks inside. He
gives a grieving sigh and does the sign of the cross.

195   **INT. RITZY HIGH-RISE/HALLWAY - NIGHT**

Jake exits the elevator.

> JAKE
> Thanks.

> ELEVATOR ATTENDANT
> You're welcome, Sir!

196   **INT. RITZY HIGH-RISE/JAKE'S APARTMENT - NIGHT**

Jake enters his apartment and flips on the lights. He walks up to
the "hole in the eyes" painting. He picks it up and stares at it...
Suddenly, he breaks it in half and shoves it in the trash. He takes
the easel, paint sets, and exits.

197   **INT. YUMI'S PLACE/LOCKER ROOM - DAY**

Jake, Sensei Yumi, and Bark enter the locker room. Jake goes to his
locker, while Yumi is a few steps away putting away equipment.

> JAKE
> My whole body aches, Sensei. Have
> anything to fix me up?

> SENSEI YUMI
> Nothing needed, except much rest.

As Jake pulls out a piece of clothing from the locker, the same key falls out and lands on the floor. Jake picks it up.

> JAKE
> Do you know where this key could be
> from? It doesn't fit anything I tried.

Yumi takes it and checks it out.

> SENSEI YUMI
> Resemble key from bus station locker.

He gives it back to him.

> JAKE
> I'll have to give it a try.

Jake sets the key back in the locker and changes his shirt.

> JAKE
> Gina told me where my mother lives.

> SENSEI YUMI
> Is good news, my son. You pay her
> visit, yes?

> JAKE
> I don't know, Sensei. I'm not so
> sure about it.

> SENSEI YUMI
> Why not sure?

> JAKE
> I did not find a single picture of
> my mother in the apartment. Neither
> of my father. I'm sure there's a
> good reason for that.

> SENSEI YUMI
> Yes, me see what you say, but she is
> family, my son. She person who gave
> you life. You must see her. Maybe it
> fill empty heart you talk about on train.

Jake ponders deeply.

198   **EXT. RUNDOWN TRAILER PARK - DUSK**

Jake pulls into a rundown trailer park. He gets out of the car and looks around. Thunder rumbles in the distance followed by lightning.

> JAKE
> Which one would it be?

He walks over to the first trailer and knocks on the door. Peggy, a SENIOR LADY in her 70's peeps through the window screen. Moments later, the door cracks open 4 inches, held by 3 security chains. Peggy speaks through the crack.

                    SENIOR LADY
              (rudely)
          Who are you, and what do you want?

                    JAKE
          Hi. I'm looking for my mother, Flora
          Daniels. You know where she lives?

                    SENIOR LADY
              (rudely)
          Never heard of her. Go away!

She slams the door. Jake walks away, but moments later, we hear the security chains coming off the door. Jake stops and looks back. The door opens wide.

                    SENIOR LADY
          Are you looking for, Flo Daniels?

                    JAKE
          Yes, I heard she lives here.

                    SENIOR LADY
          Didn't know she had a son. Try the
          black trailer by the lake. You
          can't miss it.

199   **EXT. TRASHY TRAILER PARK/FLO'S TRAILER - DUSK**

Jake pulls the Audi SUV in front of a black, Gothic feel, trailer home. He approaches the front door and knocks.

An argument brews across the street, between a man and a woman. The man angrily storms out of the house, slamming the door after him. He gets into his car and drives away squealing the tires.

Jake presses the doorbell.

                    FLO
              (from inside)
          Hold your horses, numb-nuts! I'm coming.

FLO, a Gothic looking, overly tanned, wrinkly faced, smoker's voice, woman in her 40's, opens the door, holding a cigarette between her fingers.

                    FLO
          What are you doing here, Jake?

                    JAKE
          I came to see you, Mother.

                    FLO
          What in tarnation for? I've got
          nothing to say to you.

                                                      (CONTINUED)

                              JAKE
                    I need some answers.

                              FLO
                    Why do we keep going through this? I
                    already told you I don't know who your
                    father is. I went to a party, got
                    drunk, and you came along. I know it's
                    not what you want to hear, Jake, but
                    learn to deal with it! I don't know my
                    father, and look I'm here, ain't I?

                              JAKE
                    Do I have any brothers or sisters?

                              FLO
                    For the love of god, what is the
                    matter with you!? You high on
                    something again!?

Jake swallows with grief.

                              JAKE
                    Do you believe... in God?

She chokes for a moment.

                              FLO
                         (concerned)
                    What?

                              JAKE
                    Do you believe, you know, in God?

Flo nervously takes another puff from her cigarette.

                              FLO
                    What's this about, Jake? You're
                    really starting to freak me out.

                              JAKE
                    I just need to know.

                              FLO
                    Did you suddenly become religious
                    or something? Wooooooo!

She twist-shakes both hands in the air.

                              FLO
                    You're not gonna tell me to get saved,
                    or some junk like that, are you? My
                    mother pulled that same religious voodoo
                    on me, and I hate her more now than
                    I did before she got saved. I wish I
                    never listened to her Jesus nonsense,
                    you woulda not been born, and I woulda
                    been a much happier person in life.

She takes another puff.

                                              (CONTINUED)

                         FLO
                    Too late for that, huh?

Jake sighs with a grieving heart.

                         JAKE
                    Where can I find her, my grandmother?

                         FLO
                    How should I know? 6ft under for
                    all I care.

Flo nervously takes another puff of her cigarette.

                         JAKE
                    Thank you for your time, Miss
                    Daniels. You have a good night.

                         FLO
                         (insulted)
                    "Miss Daniels!?" "Miss Daniels!?" Don't
                    give me, "Miss Daniels." This is your
                    mother who you're talking to!

Jake walks toward his SUV.

                         FLO
                    DO YOU HEAR ME, JAKE? I'M YOUR
                    MOTHER. I DEMAND YOUR RESPECT!

He drives off squealing the tires. It begins to pour.

                         FLO
                    COME HERE! COME BACK HERE RIGHT NOW!

200   **EXT. PITTSBURGH CITY ROAD - NIGHT**

      It's raining. Jake's AUDI SUV zooms by recklessly fast.

201   **INT/EXT. JAKE'S AUDI SUV - NIGHT (TRAVELING)**

      Jake swerves between cars left and right with anger. He hits
      dangerously high speeds.

      ROAD SIGN: SLOW DOWN - STEEP HILL AHEAD

      At the last second Jake slams the brakes, but doesn't make it. He
      slides down the hill and maneuvers around trees, rocks, and what
      have you. All the tires get blown out, until he finally hits a
      mound at the bottom of the hill.

202   **INT/EXT. JAKE'S AUDI SUV - NIGHT**

      It is raining. Jake's adrenaline begins to wear out. Tears

      of despair begin to roll down his face.

(CONTINUED)

                              JAKE
                    I am a nothing... A nobody. No
                    mother, no father- Nothing!... Why
                    am I even here!? Why!? I have no
                    reason to live. None!

He turns his face to God.

                              JAKE
                    God, if you're up there- If you're
                    truly up there, then talk to me.
                    Now is your chance. Show me who
                    you are. There are no second
                    chances, God. It's now or never...
                    IT'S NOW OR NEVER! DO YOU HEAR ME!?

Church music is heard coming from inside a traditional looking
Protestant church. He gets out of his car and walks closer to the
church. Jake reads the lit-up sign in front.

CHURCH SIGN: Tomorrow's Sermon by Pastor Mack - *"Do not call anyone
on earth your father; for one is your Father, He who is in heaven."*
Matthew 23:9 (NKJV)

Jake crashes to his knees and cries his broken heart to God.

203   **EXT. TRADITIONAL CHURCH - DAY**

We see a yellow taxicab approaching the church. Jake and
Sensei Yumi get out.

                              JAKE
                    That's where it happened.

Jake points out the crash site to Yumi.

                              SENSEI YUMI
                    You sure you do this, my son?

                              JAKE
                    It was God that spoke to me last
                    night. I'm sure of it.

204   **INT. TRADITIONAL CHURCH - DAY**

PASTOR MACK, a black man in his 50's, preaches a sermon. Jake and
Sensei Yumi enter and take a seat on the last bench.

The pastor tells the congregation his personal story of how he grew
up in the hood without a father, nor mother, joined a gang, got
involved with drugs, violence, sex, and so on and so forth, and how
he came to know Jesus Christ for himself.

                              PASTOR MACK
                    Matthew 10:32 says *"Therefore
                    whoever confesses Me before men,
                    him I will also confess before My
                    Father who is in heaven."* (NKJV)
                              (MORE)

                    PASTOR MACK(cont'd)
          If the Lord's word touched anyone here
          today and you would like to give your
          life to Jesus, now is your chance. Come
          forward and taste God's goodness for
          yourself. Come and be recognized. There
          is no room for shame in this place.

A few people get up and make their way down the aisle.

JAKE'S POSITION:

Moments later, Jake gets up, walks past Yumi, and down the aisle.

PASTOR MACK'S POSITION:

Jake gets to the front, along with others and they all kneel. The
pastor places his hands over them and prays. At the end the pastor
gives all of them a Bible.

205   **INT. NIGHT CLUB/BASEMENT - NIGHT**

YUMI'S POSITION:

Sensei Yumi stands in the corner with Jake at his side.

                    JAKE
          This is the last fight, Sensei. Win
          this and it's all over.

                    CLUB ANNOUNCER(O.S.)
               (overhead speakers)
          Sensei Grandpa.

CENTER RING:

Sensei Yumi gets into the center ring.

                    CLUB ANNOUNCER
               (to Sensei Yumi)
          Do you want to say anything before
          you get clobbered, Gramps?

                    SENSEI YUMI
          Yes, me say something.

Club Announcer sticks the mic in his face.

                    SENSEI YUMI
          For many weeks you see me fight biggest
          strongest foes. You think me do it from
          my own power, but me say to you, no
          victory come from my power, but God's power.
          Just like Daniel fought Goliath for God's
          glory, victory tonight will be for him.

BETTERS SECTION:

> BETTER #1
> We don't care about your God, Grandpa.

People laugh and mock him.

> BETTER #2
> GunFu is gonna murder your rear end!

> BETTER #1
> You betta believe it, sucker!

CENTER RING:

Club Announcer pulls the mic from Sensei Yumi and sticks it in
GUNFU's face, a big muscular Asian man in his 30's.

> GUNFU
> I am Goliath's brother, GunFu. You
> and your god will be crushed like a
> dirty little tin can, old man.

BOSS' POSITION:

Chork watches the fight from the VIP section along with a bunch of
other VIP Guests. Boss takes a seat beside him.

> CHORK
> Who you put your money on?

> BOSS
> GunFu, of course.

> CHORK
> Yumi.

> BOSS
> Yumi does not have a chance.

> CHORK
> He's done good for me this far.

> BOSS
> Yeah, but look at GunFu. There's no
> match. He's more than half Yumi's age,
> way stronger, and way smarter. You
> can't even compare.

Chork glaces in a certain direction and sees CHIEF VIP, an Asian man
in his 80's, with all white hair, dressed in a white suit.

> CHORK
> Did you invite him?

Chork points to Chief VIP. Panic falls on Boss' face.

> BOSS
> He wasn't due for another month?
> What's he doing here?

                         CLUB ANNOUNCER(O.S.)
                    Fighters take your places.

CENTER RING:

Yumi and GunFu face each other.

                         CLUB REFEREE
                    Ready... FIGHT!

They fight back and forth, back and forth. It seems like Yumi inches
his way toward victory.

BELL: DING-DING-DING-DING-DING!!!!!

BOSS' POSITION:

Beads of sweat pour down Boss' forehead.

                         CHORK
                    How much did you lay on him?

Boss pulls out a handkerchief and dabs his forehead.

                         BOSS
                    Way more than I should have.

YUMI'S POSITION:

Sensei Yumi comes to rest. He breathes hard.

                         SENSEI YUMI
                    Maybe they right. I too old.

                         JAKE
                    What are you talking about!? You're
                    doing great!

GUNFU'S POSITION:

                         GUNFU'S TRAINER
                    What's your problem? You're embarrassing
                    me and yourself like a total moron.

                         GUNFU
                    He's much faster than he looks.

                         GUNFU'S TRAINER
                    That's not my problem. It's yours.
                    Do whatever you gotta do, but take
                    this Jesus freak out. You got me?

GunFu doesn't answer.

                         GUNFU'S TRAINER
                    Yo!

The trainer smacks him upside his head.

                         GUNFU'S TRAINER
                    You got me!?

                              GUNFU
                    Yes, Yes. I got you. I got you.

BELL: DING-DING-DING-DING-DING!!!!!

JAKE & YUMI'S POSITION:

                              JAKE
                         (to Sensei Yumi)
                    You're on.

CENTER RING:

Yumi and GunFu line up.

                         CLUB REFEREE
                    Ready... FIGHT!

The fight goes back and forth, but this time GunFu fights harder.
He knocks Sensei Yumi to the ground hard.

JAKE'S POSITION:

                              JAKE
                    NOOOOOOOOOOOOOOOOOO!!!

CENTER RING:

Yumi is in extreme pain. The referee begins to count.

                         CLUB REFEREE
                    10, 9, 8...

Yumi tries to get up.

JAKE'S POSITION:

                              JAKE
                    STAY DOWN! STAY DOWN!

BETTERS SECTION:

                         BETTER #1
                    Where's your powerful god now, old man!?

                         BETTER #2
                    He must be on vacation. Hahahahaha!

CENTER RING:

                         CLUB REFEREE
                    5, 4, 3...

Yumi pushes himself on his fours. Referee drops the count.

GUNFU'S POSITION:

GunFu looks over at his master. His master gives him "the nod."
Emboldened with pride, GunFu heads over to Yumi.

(CONTINUED)

YUMI'S POSITION:

As soon as GunFu comes within hitting range, Yumi takes GunFu by
surprise, knocking him out cold.

JAKE'S POSITION:

> JAKE
> YES, YES, YES!!! THANK YOU, GOD!
> THANK YOU! WOOOHOOOOOOO!

VIP SECTION:

Boss leaves angry. Chork shakes his head and laughs.

CENTER RING:

The referee takes Sensei Yumi's arm and lifts it up.

> CLUB ANNOUNCER
> (overhead speakers)
> SENSEI YUMI IS OUR NEWEST CLUB
> CHAMPIOOOOOOOOOOOOOOOOOOOON!!!

Cheers rock the basement.

> SENSEI YUMI
> (to Club Announcer)
> What happened to Grandpa?

> CLUB ANNOUNCER
> Grandpa has retired and gone home.

Jake comes over to Sensei and hugs him tightly.

> JAKE
> YOU DID IT, SENSEI! YOU DID IT!

> SENSEI YUMI
> Not so hard! Not so hard! Me still
> hurting.

> JAKE
> SENSEI, YOU ARE AWESOME!!!

> SENSEI YUMI
> God is awesome, my son.

> JAKE
> That he is.

206   **INT. NIGHT CLUB/BASEMENT/BOSS' OFFICE - NIGHT**

Sensei Yumi and Jake await in Boss' office, along with Brute #1.
Boss walks in angry.

> BOSS
> What was that out there?

(CONTINUED)

CONTINUED: 180.

                         SENSEI YUMI
                    What, what?

                         BOSS
                    You made our guy look like a total
                    fool, not to mention I lost a lot
                    of my money, because of you.

                         SENSEI YUMI
                    Me not say to you, "Bet against me."

Irritated by Yumi's response, Boss pulls out a gun from the desk
drawer and sets it on top of the desk.

                         BOSS
                    You know, In most situations, I'm
                    usually a gentleman, but every
                    gentleman has their limits. What
                    was that you were saying again?
                    I didn't quite hear you.

                         SENSEI YUMI
                    Should not have bet against me, is
                    what I say.

Boss picks up the gun and points it at Yumi.

                         BOSS
                    Let's see who has the better hand
                    this time around, huh?
                         (threatening)
                    Say that again, I dare you.

Boss cocks the gun. Yumi and Jake look at one another. Jake shakes
his head in concern.

                         BOSS
                         (in Japanese)
                    C'mon, what are you waiting for?

Deep tension builds up in the room for a moment.

                         BOSS
                         (in Japanese)
                    Oh, how the tables have turned.

Chief VIP and Chork enter the room, along with CHIEF VIP'S
PERSONAL BRUTES.

                         CHIEF VIP
                    LEAVE HIM ALONE!!!

                         BOSS
                    Yumi destroyed our prized fighter.
                    He needs to pay for.

                         CHIEF VIP
                    I say, leave him alone. That
                    final. No more discussion.

                                                        (CONTINUED)

Chief VIP's Personal Brutes slowly make their way behind Boss.

                    BOSS
          I don't understand. It's what
          you would have wanted me to do.

                    CHIEF VIP
          Yumi fight with pride, with courage,
          and with honor. Something you never
          will learn sitting behind desk, with
          pen between fingers.

                    BOSS
          Who gives a rat's rear end!?
          This is a fight between Yumi
          and I. Stay out of it!

Chief VIP nods to his brutes. They take Boss down by force.

                    BOSS
          What are you doing? Let me go!

                    CHIEF VIP
          You think we not know about your
          shenanigans, do you?

                    BOSS
          What are you talking about?

                    CHIEF VIP
          We know how you build-up nice fortune
          for yourself, with our money.

                    BOSS
          I would never do that! I swear!

                    CHORK
          Oh, but you did.

Boss looks over at Chork.

                    BOSS
              (to Chork)
          Chork, you despicable little snake!
              (to Chief VIP)
          I had nothing to do with it. It was
          Chork. Chork framed me! You gotta
          believe me!

                    CHIEF VIP
          Take him away!

Two Brutes take the Boss away as he screams on the way out. Chief
VIP comes over to Sensei Yumi.

                    CHIEF VIP
          Stand up!

Jake helps Yumi stand.

                         CHIEF VIP
                    (in Japanese)
               So you are, Sensei Yumi?

                         SENSEI YUMI
                    (in Japanese)
               I am.

                         CHIEF VIP
                    (in Japanese)
               I have only heard of the legendary,
               Sensei Yumi, but now I got to see
               him for myself.

Chief VIP gives Yumi a strong manly hug.

                         CHIEF VIP
               What did for son, very honorable.
               Debt all paid. Go in peace.

Chief VIP exits first, everyone else follows. Chork takes a seat in
the Boss' chair.

                         CHORK
               Ahhhhhhh... I think I'm gonna
               enjoy this.

Yumi and Jake are just about to exit the office.

                         CHORK
               By the way, Jake!

Jake turns to face him.

                         CHORK
               I want my pen back. Don't think
               I forgot!

A moment of confusion forms on Jake's face, but then realizes what
he's referring to. Jake nods.

                         CHORK
               And Yumi!

Yumi looks directly at him.

                         CHORK
               The dust hasn't cleared between us.
               You need to pay for these scars.

Chork turns his cheek toward them.

                         SENSEI YUMI
               What you want?

                         CHORK
               I will think of something and let
               you know.

Yumi nods.

207   **EXT. NIGHT CLUB/BACK ALLEY - NIGHT**

Sensei Yumi and Jake exit the club's back alley door.

>   JAKE
>   What did he mean by that?

>   SENSEI YUMI
>   By what, my son?

>   JAKE
>   "You need to pay for these scars?"

>   SENSEI YUMI
>   These people only know money.
>   Give'm money, they go away.

>   JAKE
>   How much do you think he wants?

>   SENSEI YUMI
>   Me not know. Training tonight, yes?

>   JAKE
>   (hesitantly)
>   Uhhhhh, sure. I guess.

>   SENSEI YUMI
>   Only kidding.

Yumi laughs. Jake joins in the laughter.

>   JAKE
>   You are such a kidder, Sensei.

They chit-chat as they walk down the alley. Their voices become
gradually softer as they walk further and further.

>   SENSEI YUMI
>   We celebrate win, yes?

>   JAKE
>   Sushi?

>   SENSEI YUMI
>   Not sushi, my son. Ice Cream!!!

>   JAKE
>   Ice Cream, really!?

>   SENSEI YUMI
>   Sushi, fill belly, but Ice Cream
>   fill heart. Is important you know.

>   JAKE
>   I learn something every day.

They both turn the corner and disappear from view.

208   **EXT. PITTSBURGH PARK - DAY**

Jake sits at a park table practicing the card training. Bark
lays on the ground beside him.

                    JAKE
            6 of Hearts.

He peaks through the blindfold between cards.

                    JAKE
            Good. King of Spades... Good. 2 of
            Clover... Good. Queen of Diamonds...

A laughing couple gets Jake's attention. He removes the blindfold
to see Walking Girl running around a tree, while a HANDSOME GUY
tries to catch her. Finally, the guy catches her and they hold each
other with love and admiration. Jake looks away and sighs with grief.

                    JAKE
            Father God, I know I don't deserve
            her. I know it! (sigh) But if
            there's any way- any way at all...

Jake swallows his emotion and sighs deeply.

209   **INT. YUMI'S PLACE/KITCHEN - DAY**

Jake, Sensei Yumi, and Bark, sit at the table. 15 Poker Cards lay on
the table. Jake goes through all of them blindfolded.

                    SENSEI YUMI
            Very good, my son.

                    JAKE
            Hit me again.

Sensei Yumi quickly goes to smack him, but Jake(blindfolded)
instantly grabs his arm.

                    SENSEI YUMI
            Oh-hoooo! Reaction good too! Me come
            to think you ready. Let us see.

210   **INT. YUMI'S PLACE/DOJO - DAY (LATER)**

Jake's blindfolded. He takes a few deep breaths.

                    JAKE
                (softly to himself)
            No fear... No fear...

Sensei Yumi and Bark watch from the side. Jake takes a few more
breaths. Bark stares at him very attentively.

                    JAKE
                (softly to himself)
            No fear.

(CONTINUED)

Bark raises himself on his fours, gives off a few loud barks.
Instantly, Jake begins. Station by station, he performs all the
acrobatic moves flawlessly, just like Yumi taught him. He lands,
quickly removes the blindfold, and looks back.

                    JAKE
              (with celebration)
         WOO-HOOOOOOOOOOOOOOOOOO!!!
         I DID IT, SENSEI! I DID IT!

Bark quickly goes to Jake and celebrates.

                    JAKE
         THANK YOU, GOD!!!

Yumi deeply enjoys Jake's excitement.

                    SENSEI YUMI
         Very good, my son. Very good.

                    JAKE
         WOO-HOOOOOOOOOOOOOOOOO!!!

211   **INT. YUMI'S PLACE/LOCKER ROOM - DAY**

Jake finishes dressing. He picks up the "147" key from inside the
locker and stares at it for a moment.

212   **INT. PITTSBURGH BUS STATION/LOCKERS - DUSK**

Jake scours the bus station lockers.

                    JAKE
         147... 147. Here it is.

He sticks in the lock and twists it. It turns. He's hesitant to pull
it open, but finally does.

FROM INSIDE LOCKER:

The door opens. A duffle bag stares directly at him. He unzips the
bag and looks inside. We do not see its content. He zips it back up,
takes the bag, and closes the locker.

213   **INT. NIGHT CLUB/DANCE FLOOR ---> BASEMENT - NIGHT**

Brute #1 carries the same duffle bag through the night club. The
CLUBBERS are jamming it in the background. He walks down the basement
stairs and heads towards Boss' office, which now belongs to Chork.

214   **INT. NIGHT CLUB/BOSS' OFFICE - NIGHT**

Chork sits at his desk watching the club fight on his own Flat-screen
TV. His gun lays dismantled on the table. He cleans a piece and snaps
it together with another. He stops for a second, pulls out a little
black notebook from the desk and opens it. He picks up a thick red
marker and crosses out "Boss," which is right above "Sensei Yumi,"
then closes it.

DOOR: KNOCK-KNOCK!

> CHORK
> Yes.

Brute #1 enters and drops the duffle bag on Chork's desk.

> CHORK
> What's this?

He gives the gold pen to Chork. Chork sees "JTID" etched in.

> CHORK
> And the bag?

> BRUTE #1
> He asked me to give it to you.

Brute #1 leaves. Chork unzips the bag and finds it filled with bricks
of $100 bills. He takes one of the bricks and thumbs through it then
takes a deep sniff, and lets it out slowly as if he just got high.

Chork ponders as he feels the scars on his left cheek. He opens the
little black book again, scribbles out Yumi's name with Jake's pen,
closes the book, and sticks it back in the desk.

He picks up a cigar, clips the tip, lights it, kicks back in his
chair, and enjoys it.

215   **INT. YUMI'S PLACE/JAKE'S ROOM - NIGHT**

Jake is on the side of the bed reading the Bible. Bark is beside him.

> JAKE(V.O.)
> (James 1:23-25 (NKJV))
> *"(23) For if anyone is a hearer of the*
> *word and not a doer, he is like a man*
> *observing his natural face in a mirror;*
> *(24) for he observes himself, goes away,*
> *and immediately forgets what kind of man he*
> *was. (25) But he who looks into the perfect*
> *law of liberty and continues in it, and is*
> *not a forgetful hearer but a doer of the work,*
> *this one will be blessed in what he does."*

Jake puts the Bible down and gives a deep sigh.

> JAKE
> (softly to himself)
> Wow.

(CONTINUED)

VOCAL FAITH SONG BEGINS...

He kneels beside the bed and prays silently. After a moment Jake
looks up the white canvas that sits in his room.

                                                          CUT TO:

Jake places some paint on the slab, picks up a paintbrush, thinks
for a moment, and starts painting.

216   **YUMI'S PLACE/JAKE'S ROOM - NIGHT (PAINTING MONTAGE)**

We see a super close up montage of Jake's new creation. Brush stroke,
after brush stroke, after brush stroke...

217   **INT. YUMI'S PLACE/JAKE'S ROOM - MORNING**

Jake puts the last touch on the painting. He takes a breath and
releases it slowly. He backs up and stares at it.

                            JAKE
                  This is my best work.

Bark jumps off the bed and sees the painting. He immediately begins
to howl. It's an magnificent portrait of Gracie with her long
flowing hair, hugging Bark. Bark continues to howl. Jake gets down
on his knees and holds Bark.

218   **INT. JACOBS' HOUSE/GRACIE'S ROOM - DAY**

An elegant Amish wedding dress lays on the bed. We slowly pan to
Gracie who is on her knees praying on the side of the bed, with
sorrowful tears pouring down her face.

NEAR THE DOOR:

Mrs. Jacobs walks by Gracie's room and sees Gracie praying. Tears
begin to pour down her face. She wipes them off with her hand. After
a moment she leaves.

VOCAL FAITH SONG ENDS.

219   **INT. JACOBS' HOUSE/BACK PORCH - DAY**

Mr. Jacobs sits on a porch chair gazing out at the fully-grown crop
fields, the fields Jake has helped plant. Mrs. Jacobs exits the
house and takes a seat beside him.

                        MRS. JACOBS
                  What are we doing, Mr. Jacobs?...
                  It is not right that Gracie should
                  carry our burdens.

Mr. Jacobs gives a deep sigh.

                        MRS. JACOBS
                  We should tell her the truth, and
                  let her decide our fate.

                                                      (CONTINUED)

He holds her tightly and gives another sigh. Gracie exits the house.

> GRACIE
> (with courage)
> I have decided that I will not marry
> Caleb. You can force me to do whatever
> you want, but you cannot force me to
> say "yes" to him. I love Isaac and I
> will not betray my love for him by
> saying "yes" to a man whom I do not
> love. I will not do it!

Mr. Jacobs and Mrs. Jacobs stare at one another with love and compassion. He gives Mrs. Jacobs a nod.

> MR. JACOBS
> Come, my daughter, have a seat. We have
> something very important to tell you.

Gracie takes a seat across from them.

> MR. JACOBS
> We will share a secret with you. After
> you have heard it, you may do what your
> heart desires. The decision you make,
> we will both respect.

> GRACIE
> Tell me, Father.

Moment of silence as he ponders.

> MR. JACOBS
> You, my daughter, are only half Amish.

> GRACIE
> (confused)
> Half Amish? I do not understand.

Mrs. Jacobs takes Mr. Jacobs' hand and looks directly into her eyes with love and admiration.

> MR. JACOBS
> Your mother is Amish, but I am not.
> I am of the English.

Moment of silence as Gracie takes it in.

> MR. JACOBS
> Caleb discovered the truth and used it
> against us. He said if I do not hand you
> to him, he will confess it to everyone.

Gracie gets teary-eyed, then suddenly collapses>>>

> GRACIE
> Oh, Father!

>>>in her father's arms with grief.

> GRACIE
> I do not want to marry that man.

220   **EXT. AERIAL VIEW OF DOWNTOWN DETROIT - DAY**

We see a riverfront aerial view of Downtown Detroit.

                    COMMENTATOR TY(V.O.)
          We are in Detroit, Michigan at the
          Final Round of Competitions. Where
          the East meets the West.>>>

221   **INT. DETROIT ARENA/FLOOR/COMMENTATOR'S POSITION - DAY**

                    COMMENTATOR TY
          >>>Where today the last man
          standing will take home the
          National Championship Trophy and a
          grand prize of $100,000.

                    COMMENTATOR DAVE
          Many fighters have come and gone,
          and the ones left standing are the
          cream of the crop, in so few words.

222   **INT. DETROIT ARENA/LOCKER ROOM - DAY**

Jake finishes getting dressed for the fight. He sits down on
the bench terribly nervous.

Sensei Yumi walks in.

                    SENSEI YUMI
          Today big-big day, my son! How feeling?

                    JAKE
          My stomach is turning inside out.

                    SENSEI YUMI
          Means you fine.

                    JAKE
          I don't want to be afraid, but I'm
          fighting the best of the best.

                    SENSEI YUMI
          Yes, no doubt very good fighters on floor,
          but remember, my son. They also fear you.

                    JAKE
          I overheard some people talking about
          a fighter named, Buzz-Cut. They said he
          won the championship 3 years in a row.

                    SENSEI YUMI
          Yes, me know him, and he full of air, if
          ask me. No concern yourself, my son. We
          deal with him when time comes. Okay?

                    JAKE
          Okay.

                                              (CONTINUED)

Sensei hands Jake a present wrapped in Christmas wrapping.

                    SENSEI YUMI
          Here, early Christmas present.

Jake takes it.

                    JAKE
          What is it?

                    SENSEI YUMI
          Open and see.

He tears open the wrapping. It's the Warrior's Uniform.

                    JAKE
          Oh, wow-o-wow!

                    SENSEI YUMI
          Before Mrs. go to the Lord, she have me
          promise to give uniform to fighter with
          pure heart, and you, my son, fighter
          with pure heart.

                    JAKE
          I cannot believe this! Oh, wow! It was
          magnificent in the case, but holding
          it in my hands is even more magnificent-
          but you sure I deserve this, Sensei?
          I must've been your worst student.

                    SENSEI YUMI
          Naaaaa, you not worst student. I
          had much worser ones than you.

They both laugh lightly.

                    JAKE
                (sarcastically)
          Ok, thanks!

                    SENSEI YUMI
          Have plans if win grand prize?

                    JAKE
          Oh, wow! I don't know. I haven't
          really thought about it.

                    SENSEI YUMI
          But if win, what you do?

                    JAKE
          Well... I'd like to move somewhere
          where it's quiet. I don't know. Maybe
          buy a cattle ranch. I'm not sure. Of
          course, that's if we win. How 'bout
          you? You have any plans?

                    SENSEI YUMI
          Me want to leave city after Mrs. pass away,
          but never get chance. Now me get chance.

                                                          (CONTINUED)

DETROIT STAFF LADY, a female in her 40's, enters.

                    DETROIT STAFF LADY
          You're needed in 15.

                    SENSEI YUMI
          We be there in 10.
                    (to Jake)
          Remember, my son. Take picture,
          STRIKE, eyes closed. Fight like
          you won. Also, 2 timeouts for
          every match. If knocked on floor,
          me cannot call timeout till
          get on all fours. Got it?

                    JAKE
          Got it.

                    SENSEI YUMI
          Good. Come, I pray.

They bow their head. Sensei Yumi does the sign of the cross.

223   **INT. SHERIFF PHIL'S HOME/LIVING ROOM - DAY**

Sheriff Phil watches the karate fight with Marcus.

                    SHERIFF PHIL
                    (louder)
          Anya, Keesha! It's about to start.

                    MARCUS
          Go Isaac, Go! You can do it!

ANYA(upper 30's), an attractive black woman with a slight Jamaican
accent, enters with KEESHA(mid teens), their daughter.

                    KEESHA
          Make room for us!

DOOR BELL: DING-DONG!

                    ANYA
          Who could that be?

224   **EXT. SHERIFF PHIL'S HOME/FRONT DOOR - DAY**

Sheriff Phil opens the door. Timmy, Amish Teen #1, and Amish Teen #2
are standing at the door.

                    TIMMY
          Good day, Sir. My name is Timmy and
          we were wondering, if we could,
          possibly, maybe...

They stare at each other in shame.

225   **INT. DETROIT ARENA MONTAGE - DAY**

We see a montage of Jake climbing up the competition ladder. This
montage is intercut with a sub-montage of BUZZ-CUT, a bald white man
in his 20's, with tattoos and body rings all over the place, and
a braided long beard. He ruthlessly fights opponent after opponent,
winning fight after fight.

226   **INT. SHERIFF PHIL'S HOME/LIVING ROOM - NIGHT**

Sheriff Phil, Marcus, Keesha, Timmy, Amish Teen #1, Amish Teen #2
watch the fight. Anya enters with bags of popcorn.

                    ANYA
          Popcorn anyone?

                    AMISH TEEN #1
          I would like one.

                    AMISH TEEN #2
          Yes, please.

She hands them the bags.

          AMISH TEEN #1   AMISH TEEN #2
Thank you!   Thank you!

Timmy gives them no-no look.

                    ANYA
          Would you like one too, Timmy?

                    TIMMY
          Yes, thank you.

The other two look over at him and give him a no-no look.

                    TIMMY
          What!? She offered!

DOOR BELL: DING-DONG!

227   **INT. SHERIFF PHIL'S HOME/FRONT DOOR - NIGHT**

Sheriff Phil opens the door and finds more AMISH BOYS from
Jake's class, twiddling their thumbs and embarrassed to talk.

228   **INT. DETROIT ARENA - NIGHT**

COMMENTATOR'S POSITION:

                    COMMENTATOR DAVE
          What an exciting night, Ty. What an
          exciting night!!!

                                        (CONTINUED)

                         COMMENTATOR TY
                    (to Dave)
               You said it, Dave.
                    (to Audience)
               We're down to our last two
               fighters in the East Division Finals.
               "The Ice" Daniels and Trane. Both
               fighters have gone through tremendous
               hurdles to get here, especially Jake
               Daniels, whom I understand has lost
               his memory due to a tragic accident
               he faced months back.

                         COMMENTATOR DAVE
                    (to Ty)
               Which explains his long absence
               from the tournament.

                         COMMENTATOR TY
                    (to Dave)
               It sure does.
                    (to audience)
               One of these two fighters, either
               Daniels, or Trane will face the
               undefeated three year in-a-row
               returning champion, Buzz-Cut, and
               the way he's been fighting tonight,
               it doesn't look like he's about to
               give up the trophy any time soon.

                         COMMENTATOR DAVE
               They're lining up. Let's go to the floor.

CENTER FLOOR:

TRANE, a Japanese man in his 20's, and JAKE take the floor.

                         DETROIT REFEREE
               Face each other... Bow... FIGHT!

They circle around each other for a moment. Jake goes for a hit,
Trane backs off behind the fight line. DETROIT REFEREE, an Asian man
in his 50's, blows the whistle. They align for another round.

                         DETROIT REFEREE
               Face each other... Bow... FIGHT!

Again they circle around each other for a moment and again Jake goes
for a hit. Again TRANE exits the fight line.

TRANE'S COACH calls a time out.

SENSEI YUMI'S POSITION:

Jake comes to SENSEI YUMI.

                         JAKE
               He doesn't want to fight me,
               Sensei. I can feel it.

                                                      (CONTINUED)

Yumi observes the interaction between Trane, TRANE'S PARENTS, and TRANE'S COACH, as an argument brews between them. Trane's coach throws in the towel and leaves angry.

                    SENSEI YUMI
          I sense fear in Trane's eyes, my son.

                    JAKE
          Fear of what? Of me?

                    SENSEI YUMI
          No, not you.

                    DETROIT ANNOUNCER (O.S.)
              (overhead speakers)
          Fighters take your places.

                    JAKE
          Gotta go.

Jake leaves. Yumi looks over at Buzz-Cut.

CENTER FLOOR:

Jake and Trane take the floor.

                    TRANE
          Sensei Yumi is a real legend in our
          country. Would you introduce us after
          the competition?

                    JAKE
          Sure. It would be my pleasure.

                    TRANE
          Thank you. I greatly appreciate it.

Detroit Referee comes in.

                    DETROIT REFEREE
              (to Trane)
          Step outside the fight line one more
          time and you'll be disqualified.

                    TRANE
              (to referee)
          I am forfeiting the match.

                    DETROIT REFEREE
          You sure? There's no going back.

                    TRANE
          I am sure.

                    DETROIT REFEREE
          Okay. I'll let the judges know.

Detroit Referee leaves.

                    JAKE
          Why?

(CONTINUED)

                              TRANE
                    Have you seen Buzz-Cut fight? He's
                    a mad man. He already put 2 fighters
                    in the hospital and I don't care to
                    be his 3rd. I wish you the best of
                    luck, Jake Daniels. I pray you beat
                    him. He deserves to be beat.

Trane bows to Jake. Jake returns the bow. Trane leaves.

Jake looks over at Buzz-Cut, who gives him a deep cold stare. Jake
swallows with concern.

229   **INT. SHERIFF PHIL'S HOME/LIVING ROOM - NIGHT**

Sheriff Phil, his family, and all the Amish Boys watch the fight.

                         DETROIT ANNOUNCER(TV)
                    Trane forfeits the match. Jake
                    Daniels becomes the East Division
                    Champion by default.

Everyone in the house celebrates.

                           AMISH TEEN #2
                         (to everyone)
                    We need more brothers like Trane.
                    He is nice.

DOOR BELL: DING-DONG!

230   **INT. SHERIFF PHIL'S HOME/FRONT DOOR - NIGHT**

Sheriff Phil opens the door. It's Gracie and Abe.

                          ALL AMISH BOYS
                         (to Gracie & Abe)
                    Heyyyyyyyyyyyyyyyyyy!!!!

                          SHERIFF PHIL
                    It's about time you two showed up.

231   **INT. DETROIT ARENA - NIGHT**

COMMENTATOR'S POSITION:

                         DETROIT ANNOUNCER
                         (overhead speakers)
                    Welcome to the National Championship
                    finale. This is what we've all been
                    waiting for. On my right, Jake "The
                    Ice" Daniels.

Crowd cheers.

                                                        (CONTINUED)

                    DETROIT ANNOUNCER
              And on my left, Buzz-Cut.

Cheers, with some light boos.

                    DETROIT ANNOUNCER
              Fighters have 5 minutes to make
              their final preparations.

SENSEI YUMI'S POSITION:

Sensei Yumi checks the board. Jake enters.

                    JAKE
              He's staring at me, Sensei.

Sensei Yumi takes off the old karate bandage.

                    SENSEI YUMI
              No look.

                    JAKE
              Why is he staring at me?

                    SENSEI YUMI
              He try to mess with mind, but you
              no let him.

Yumi puts on the new bandage.

                    JAKE
              He sure looks mean.

                    SENSEI YUMI
              Ugly form of intimidation, but no
              be afraid of what outside. Inside
              what important. Come, I say prayer.

They bow their heads.

                    SENSEI YUMI
              Father God...

BUZZ-CUT'S POSITION:

BUZZ-CUT'S MASTER, an older, rough looking man, approaches Buzz-Cut.

                    BUZZ-CUT'S MASTER
              Awwwwwww, now isn't that cute.
              They're praying to their god.

They laugh.

                    BUZZ-CUT'S MASTER
              Just keep doing what you're doing and
              we'll be getting drunk tonight. My treat!

His teacher gives him a pat on the back.

                    BUZZ-CUT
              Yes, Master.

                                                    (CONTINUED)

JAKE'S POSITION:

Sensei Yumi and Jake finish praying.

>   SENSEI YUMI
>   Help him fight for your honor and
>   your glory. In your Son's name, Amen.

>   JAKE
>   Amen.

>   SENSEI YUMI
>   If lose, lose for God, and if win, win
>   for God, so no matter if lose, or win,
>   the fight is God's. Remember that.

>   JAKE
>   I will.

>   DETROIT ANNOUNCER
>   (overhead speakers)
>   Fighters take your positions.

>   SENSEI YUMI
>   After competition, Me no more be your
>   Sensei, my son. Me retiring for good.

Jake becomes teary eyed.

>   JAKE
>   You've been like a father to me, Sensei.
>   Don't ever stop being my father.

Yumi becomes teary eyed and gives Jake an encouraging hug.

>   SENSEI YUMI
>   Me love you like son. No stop
>   being my son.

COMMENTATOR'S POSITION:

>   COMMENTATOR DAVE
>   This' what we've all been waiting
>   for. We are moments away from the
>   last fight of the night. The
>   anticipation is simply breathtaking.

>   COMMENTATOR TY
>   Our fighters are lining up.
>   Let the action begin.

CENTER FLOOR:

Jake and Buzz-Cut are lined up for the fight.

>   DETROIT REFEREE
>   Face each other... Bow... FIGHT!

Immediately, Buzz-Cut goes after Jake. Jake exits the fight line.
They take their places once again.

                        DETROIT REFEREE
                Face each other... Bow... FIGHT!

Buzz-Cut immediately goes for another strike, but Jake strikes back,
pushing him outside the fight line. Buzz-Cut goes after Jake as if
he's going to get into a street fight.

232   **INT. SHERIFF PHIL'S HOME/LIVING ROOM - NIGHT**

        Everyone at Phil's home boos with the crowd.

                        COMMENTATOR DAVE(TV)
                10-point misconduct penalty for
                Buzz-Cut.

233   **INT. DETROIT ARENA - NIGHT**

        CENTER FLOOR:

        Detroit Referee approaches Buzz-Cut.

                        DETROIT REFEREE
                    (to Buzz-Cut)
                You will fight by the rules or
                forfeit. Understand!?

                        BUZZ-CUT
                Whatever!

        Once again, they take their places.

                        DETROIT REFEREE
                Face each other... Bow... FIGHT!

        The fight goes back and forth. They both get beat up pretty intense.
        In the end, Jake gets knocked down to the ground.

        *******************************SLOW MOTION*******************************

        Jake's head spins. The Referee begins the count.

        ****************************BACK TO NORMAL****************************

234   **INT. SHERIFF PHIL'S HOME/LIVING ROOM - NIGHT**

        Everyone watching are on the edge of their seats. With tears in her
        eyes, Gracie prays silently in her heart.

235   **INT. DETROIT ARENA - NIGHT**

        CENTER FLOOR:

        A sudden strength comes over him and he gets up on all fours.

        YUMI'S POSITION:

        YUMI quickly calls a time out.

236   **INT. DETROIT ARENA/MEDICAL ROOM - NIGHT**

Jake lays flat on the bed. Sensei Yumi stands beside him, along with the HEAD MEDICAL GUY, a man in his 50's.

> HEAD MEDICAL GUY
> You're a lucky man. Nothing seems to
> be broken, but your left arm has been
> dislocated. I suggest you withdraw.

> JAKE
> No, you gotta put it back.

> HEAD MEDICAL GUY
> You'll have to go to the hospital
> for that. Sorry.

> SENSEI YUMI
> (to Head Medical Guy)
> Thank you. We see what we do.

Medical staff leaves.

> JAKE
> Put it back, Sensei? I don't want
> to go down like this.

> SENSEI YUMI
> Go down like what, my son?

> JAKE
> Like this. It's not right.

> SENSEI YUMI
> Why you need to defeat him? Me already
> very proud of you. Why need this?

> JAKE
> Because I can defeat him, and he
> needs to be defeated. I don't
> know why, but he needs to be.

Yumi ponders for a long while.

> JAKE
> I can do this, Sensei. I know it!

Yumi ponders some more.

> SENSEI YUMI
> No doubt opponent very good...
> but... opponent have flaw.

> JAKE
> What flaw, tell me?

> SENSEI YUMI
> Opponent flaw is teacher.

> JAKE
> Teacher?

(CONTINUED)

                    SENSEI YUMI
          Student do what teacher say, yes?

                    JAKE
          I guess so.

                    SENSEI YUMI
          Teacher have prideful heart. Use
          to your advantage.

                    JAKE
          How?

                    SENSEI YUMI
          Fight with mind, my son.

Detroit Staff Lady opens the door and speaks through it.

                    DETROIT STAFF LADY
          There's a call for Jake on Line 4.

                    JAKE
          I can't talk to anyone right now.

                    DETROIT STAFF LADY
          I don't know. It seems pretty-pretty
          important. I think you should take it.

                    JAKE
              (to Sensei Yumi)
          Would you go see who it is?

                    SENSEI YUMI
          Okay, but let's fix arm first.
              (to Detroit Staff Lady)
          Tell them, 2 minutes.

                    DETROIT STAFF LADY
          Will do.

She leaves. Yumi feels around Jake's left shoulder.

                    SENSEI YUMI
          Me see problem. This will hurt, sorry.

                    JAKE
          Do it!

Jake tries to hold in the pain. Yumi thrusts his arm back into place.

                    SENSEI YUMI
          There, arm good as new.

                    JAKE
              (with pain)
          Boy, did that ever hurt!

                    SENSEI YUMI
          Good pain is good. Me go see
          who on phone.

Yumi leaves.

237   **INT. SHERIFF PHIL'S HOME/KITCHEN - NIGHT**

Gracie's on the phone. Anya is beside her.

                    SENSEI YUMI(V.O.)
                (on phone)
            Hello?

                    GRACIE
            Hi, my name is Gracie, Gracie Jacobs.

238   **INT. DETROIT ARENA/MEDICAL ROOM - NIGHT**

Jake's on the bed. DETROIT STAFF MAN(mid 50's) enters.

                    DETROIT STAFF MAN
            5 minutes to get back, or forfeit.

                    JAKE
                (sigh) Thanks.

Staff Man leaves. Jake gets down on his knees, on the side of
the bed, and painfully brings his hands together.

                    JAKE
            Lord, this is your fight. Tell me
            what to do.

239   **INT. DETROIT ARENA/FLOOR - NIGHT**

                    COMMENTATOR DAVE
            30 more seconds and Buzz-Cut will
            be this year's National Champion.

CROWD GOES WILD!!!

                    COMMENTATOR TY
            What's this?!

240   **INT. DETROIT ARENA - NIGHT**

Jake walks into the arena limping badly on his right foot.

                    COMMENTATOR DAVE(V.O.)
            He's back, Folks! "The Ice" is back!
            He's going to fight!

COMMENTATOR'S POSITION:

                    COMMENTATOR TY
            You know, Dave, we gave him that name,
            but it just doesn't seem to fit him
            anymore.

                    COMMENTATOR DAVE
            You're absolutely right, Ty. How
            about, "The Nice?"

(CONTINUED)

                         COMMENTATOR TY
                    "The Nice?"

                         COMMENTATOR DAVE
                    Sure, why not?

Ty ponders for a tad.

                         COMMENTATOR TY
                    It's a little cheesy, but I like it!
                    Someone needs to tell the announcer.

241   **INT. DETROIT ARENA/PHONE - NIGHT**

Sensei Yumi's on the phone.

                         SENSEI YUMI
                    I will make sure to let him know,
                    Gracie. Bye-bye.

242   **INT. DETROIT ARENA - NIGHT**

JAKE'S POSITION:

Jake badly limps on his leg. He gazes over at his opponent.

                         COMMENTATOR DAVE(V.O.)
                    Looks like Jake's right leg is
                    giving him some trouble.

                         COMMENTATOR TY(V.O.)
                    No doubt Buzz-Cut will use that to
                    his advantage.

Sensei Yumi enters the scene.

                         SENSEI YUMI
                    Why limping? Leg bad too?

                         JAKE
                    I'm fighting with my mind, like you
                    taught me... I just hope it works.

BUZZ-CUT'S POSITION:

                         BUZZ-CUT'S MASTER
                    Shoot for the leg and end this
                    thing already.

                         BUZZ-CUT
                    Yes, Master.

                         DETROIT REFEREE(V.O.)
                         (over the speakers)
                    Fighters, take your places.

Buzz-Cut gets up to leave.

                                                        (CONTINUED)

                         BUZZ-CUT'S MASTER
                    Show him who's boss!

Buzz-Cut nods with a arrogant smile and leaves.

CENTER RING:

Jake and Buzz-Cut take their places on the floor. Jake limps
the whole entire time.

                         COMMENTATOR DAVE(V.O.)
                    I'm not sure how he'll be able to
                    fight with that leg.

                         COMMENTATOR TY(V.O.)
                    It is going to be interesting to see
                    how this will go down, but I don't
                    see it, Dave. I don't see it going
                    too well for Jake "The Ice," I mean,
                    "The Nice" Daniels.

                         DETROIT REFEREE
                    Face each other... Bow... FIGHT!

Jake limps around the floor for a moment. Finally Buzz-Cut goes for
the kill, aiming directly for Jake's right leg, but Jake uses his
right leg to do an awesome maneuver, with a direct hit to Buzz-Cut's
face, knocking him down to the ground. The referee counts down.

                         COMMENTATOR DAVE(V.O.)
                    UTTERLY UNBELIEVABLE, FOLKS! I CANNOT
                    FIND THE WORDS TO EXPRESS WHAT I'VE
                    JUST SEEN WITH MY VERY OWN EYES!
                    UNBELIEVABLE! WHERE'S THAT REPLAY!?

TV REPLAY: Slow motion replay of Jake hitting Buzz-Cut.

                         COMMENATOR TY(V.O.)
                    Just look at that form! I've never
                    seen anything like it! Are his eyes
                    closed? Zoom in on the eyes.

TV replay zooms on Jake's eyes.

              COMMENATOR TY(V.O.) & COMMENTATOR DAVE(V.O.)
                         NO WAYYYYYYYYYY!!!

COMMENTATOR'S POSITION:

                         COMMENTATOR DAVE(V.O)
                    Jake Daniels fooled Buzz-Cut into
                    thinking his right leg was injured,
                         (to Ty)
                    but is that even legal, Ty?

                         COMMENTATOR TY(V.O.)
                    Perfectly legal. It's called, fighting
                    with your mind.

CONTINUED: 204.

CENTER FLOOR:

At the last second Buzz-Cut finds the strength to stand on his fours.
Buzz-Cut's teacher calls for a time out. Jake holds his arm in pain
as he leaves the floor.

YUMI'S POSITION:

Jake comes over to Sensei Yumi holding his left arm in pain.

> SENSEI YUMI
> Very good, my son! Very good.

> JAKE
> I can barely move my arm, Sensei.
> Is there anything you can do?

Yumi massages Jake's arm as he bends it in different
directions. Jake holds in the pain.

> SENSEI YUMI
> How feel?

> JAKE
> It's the same

243 **INT. SHERIFF PHIL'S HOME/LIVING ROOM - NIGHT**

> COMMENTATOR DAVE(TV)
> I hate to say it, but it looks like
> Jake is done for.

> COMMENTATOR TY(TV)
> The truth hurts sometimes. Buzz-Cut
> will not fall for that again.

244 **INT. DETROIT ARENA - NIGHT**

JAKE AND YUMI'S POSITION:

Sensei Yumi continues to massage Jake's arm as he bends it in
different directions.

> SENSEI YUMI
> How 'bout now?

> JAKE
> No, it's still the same... I don't
> want to call it quits, but I can't
> possibly fool him twice.

> SENSEI YUMI
> No need to fool. Let him hit you.

Confusion forms on Jake's face.

> JAKE
> Let him do what?

(CONTINUED)

                    SENSEI YUMI
          Let him hit you, my son. Let him
          hit you in bad arm.

Jake's ponders for a moment, then suddenly...

                    JAKE
          Do you mean like--

                    SENSEI YUMI
          Yes, exactly what I mean.

BUZZ-CUT'S POSITION:

The Head Medical Guy works to stop Buzz-Cut's bloody nose. Buzz-Cut's
Master enters.

                    BUZZ-CUT'S MASTER
                (with rudeness)
          Get your hands off him. He's fine!

Head Medical Guy leaves.

                    BUZZ-CUT'S MASTER
                (to Buzz-Cut)
          Now listen to me, and listen to me good.
          You're gonna go out there and finish him
          off, like I taught you. Do you hear me!?

                    BUZZ-CUT
          Yes, Master.

                    BUZZ-CUT'S MASTER
          Go for that left arm, and the rest is
          history. He fooled us once, but he won't
          fool us twice, and don't- and I do mean
          don't, disappoint me.

                    BUZZ-CUT
          Yes, Master.

JAKE'S POSITION:

Deep worry shows on Jake's face.

                    JAKE
          I'm so dreading this, Sensei. Isn't
          there another way?

                    SENSEI YUMI
          In life, some decisions easy, and some
          decisions hard... This one hard, my son.

Jake mulls over Yumi's advice.

                    JAKE
          You think it'll work?

                    SENSEI YUMI
          You believe in miracles?

Jake ponders for a moment.

                    JAKE
          It's a miracle we're here.

Yumi nods.

                    SENSEI YUMI
          That it is, my son. That it is. But
          one thing even more miracle?

                    JAKE
          What?

Moment of silence.

                    SENSEI YUMI
          She watching you, my son.

A look of confusion forms on Jake's face.

                    JAKE
          Who? Who's watching me?

                    SENSEI YUMI
          Your girl. She watching on TV.

                    JAKE
          Who, Gracie?

                    SENSEI YUMI
          Yes. I speak to her on phone.

                    JAKE
          That was Gracie on the phone?

                    JAKE
          Yes, my son.

An expression of joy and happiness forms on his face.

                    JAKE
              (with excitement)
          What did she say!? Tell me!

                    SENSEI YUMI
          Tomorrow her wedding day. She say
          she not marry him if... If you go
          for her. She marry you.

                    JAKE
          Really, she said that?

                    SENSEI YUMI
          Yes.

Jake becomes teary eyed with emotions.

                    SENSEI YUMI
          You go, yes?

                          DETROIT ANNOUNCER
                          (overhead speakers)
                     Fighters take your positions!

                          SENSEI YUMI
                     You go for girl, yes, my son?

Jake gives a deep sigh and fixes his composure.

                          JAKE
                     I wouldn't miss it for the world.
                     Let's take down Goliath.

CENTER FLOOR:

Buzz-Cut is on the floor waiting. Jake comes in.

                          BUZZ-CUT
                          (to Jake)
                     I have had it up to here with your
                     games! You're going down! No more mercy!

COMMENTATOR DAVE(V.O.)

                     What is Jake planning on doing?

COMMENTATOR TY(V.O.)

                     I have no idea.

                          DETROIT REFEREE
                     Face each other... Bow... FIGHT!

*******************************SLOW MOTION*******************************

Buzz-Cut goes for Jake's arm, taking him down instantly.

****************************BACK TO NORMAL****************************

Buz-Cut declares himself the winner. The crowd boos.

                          BUZZ-CUT
                          (arrogantly)
                     YEAHHHHHH! YEAHHHHHH! THAT IS HOW
                     YOU DO IT RIGHT THERE! YEAHHHHHH!
                          (to crowd)
                     BOO TO YOU, LOSERS!

On the floor, Jake holds his arm in excruciating pain.

245   **INT. SHERIFF PHIL'S HOME/LIVING ROOM - NIGHT**

Everyone at Phil's home is saddened with grief.

                          GRACIE
                          (to everyone)
                     He needs our prayers.

                          ABE
                     Yes... Yes he does.

All the Amish hold hands and begin to pray in their hearts.

246   **JAKES PRARIE DAYDREAM**

Jake's lifeless body lays in the middle of a prairie field filled
with flowers. Gracie, leans over his body and kisses him on the
lips. Within seconds, Jake opens his eyes and takes a deep breath.

                                                        CUT TO:

247   **INT. DETROIT ARENA - NIGHT**

A surge strength comes over Jake's body, pushing himself on
all fours. Detroit Referee immediately stops the countdown.

                    COMMENTATOR TY(V.O.)
               Why doesn't Yumi call a
               time-out? He has one left.

Buzz-Cut peers over at his Master. His Master give him the
"slice-throat" signal. With guard down, Buzz-Cut approaches Jake
arrogantly to finish him off, but as soon as Buzz-Cut comes within
range, Jake makes a surprising, closed-eyed acrobatic maneuver,
taking Buzz-Cut down hard. Same maneuver Yumi used on GunFu when
they fought.

COMMENTATOR'S POSITION:

                    COMMENTATOR DAVE
               THIS IS UTTERLY UNBELIEVABLE! OUT OF
               THIS WORLD, INCREDIBLE! JAKE DANIELS
               PULLED ANOTHER FAST ONE ON BUZZ-CUT.

                    COMMENTATOR TY
               I HAVE NEVER SEEN THIS KIND OF
               FIGHTING TECHNIQUE IN MY 25 YEARS
               OF BEING IN THIS TOURNAMENT. IT'S
               OFF THE WALL AMAZING, DAVE!

CENTER FLOOR:

                    DETROIT REFEREE
               3, 2, 1.

DETROIT ANNOUNCER

                    (overhead speakers)
               AND OUR NEW NATIONAL CHAMPION IS
               JAKE "THE NIIIIIIIICE" DANIELS!

And the crowd goes wild!!!

248   **INT. SHERIFF PHIL'S HOME/LIVING ROOM - NIGHT**

Everyone celebrates Jake's win with cheers and hugs.

209.

249   **INT. DETROIT ARENA - NIGHT**

Detroit Announcer comes to Jake with a wireless hand-held mic.

>   DETROIT ANNOUNCER
>   Tell us a little something about your
>   victory tonight, Jake Daniels.

Jake takes the mic from him and begins to get teary-eyed.

>   JAKE
>   (with emotion)
>   Oh, man!... I think I've got something
>   in my eyes.

The audience gives a slight laugh. Jake fixes his composure.

>   JAKE
>   Firstly, God deserves the credit for my
>   victory tonight. If it weren't for him, I
>   would not be standing in front of you right
>   now. With that said, my Sensei, Sensei Yumi,
>   who has selflessly taken me into his home
>   and made me his second son.

>   JAKE
>   (to Sensei Yumi)
>   Thank you, Sensei!

Sensei Yumi gives Jake a side hug. Audience roars.

>   JAKE
>   If you ever need a good rear kicking,
>   Sensei Yumi is your man... Without a doubt.

250   **INT. SHERIFF PHIL'S HOME/LIVING ROOM - NIGHT**

TV audience laughs along with everyone at Phil's home.

>   JAKE(TV)
>   I would also like to thank someone
>   who's been there through thick and
>   thin... My best friend, Bark, my dog.

251   **INT. DETROIT ARENA - NIGHT**

>   JAKE(TV)
>   And Yes, that's his name. It's a long
>   story. Don't ask.

252   **INT. YUMI'S PLACE/MUSEUM ROOM - NIGHT**

>   JAKE(TV)
>   (to Bark)
>   Thank you, Bark! I'll be home soon.

Bark barks, as he watches Jake's live speech.

253   **INT. DETROIT ARENA - NIGHT**

Holding the mic, Jake begins to get teary-eyed once again.

                    JAKE
          There must be something in the air.
          I don't know what it is.

Jake fixes his composure once again.

                    JAKE
          In conclusion, I would like to say
          something to someone very-very special-
          someone very dear to my heart. My lovely
          angel, Gracie Jacobs, the love of my life.>>>

254   **INT. SHERIFF PHIL'S HOME/LIVING ROOM - NIGHT**

                    JAKE(TV)
                 (into the camera)
          >>>Gracie. These past few months have
          been like a fish out of water. I
          cannot live without you any longer.>>>

255   **INT. DETROIT ARENA - NIGHT**

                    JAKE
          >>>I love you and will always love you,
          till I close my eyes on this Earth.>>>

256   **INT. SHERIFF PHIL'S HOME/LIVING ROOM - NIGHT**

Tears run down Gracie's face.

                    JAKE
          >>>Be forever mine, because my heart
          is already forever yours.

A jolt of emotions comes over Gracie. She wipes her tears.

257   **INT. DETROIT ARENA - NIGHT**

                    JAKE
          Don't marry him, Gracie. I am coming
          for you, just don't say, "yes." I will
          be there tomorrow. I love you!

Jake gives the mic back. Cheers rock the stadium.

258   **INT. SHERIFF PHIL'S HOME/LIVING ROOM - NIGHT**

Gracie gets closer to the TV and puts her hand on Jake. Tears of
happiness flow down her face.

                    GRACIE
                 (mouth w/o voice)
          And I love you.

259   **INT. DETROIT ARENA - NIGHT**

Jake, Trane, and Trane's Parents come over to Sensei Yumi. Jake's
left hand is bandaged around his neck.

                    JAKE
          Sensei, I want you to meet Trane.

Trane bows.

                    TRANE
              (in Japanese)
          Greetings Sensei. My name is Chi and
          these are my parents. It is a privilege
          and honor to finally meet you in person.

                    SENSEI YUMI
              (in Japanese)
          Thank you. It is an honor to meet you.

JAKE'S POSITION:

Jake stands back and admires Sensei Yumi. He looks up and fist-bumps
his heart and points up.

                    JAKE
              (mouth w/o voice)
          Thank you.

Suddenly, Jake is rushed by people who want to meet/greet him too.

260   **EXT. JACOBS' FARM - DAY**

Both in their wedding attire, Gracie and Caleb stand before Father
Bishop who is reciting the ceremony.

Gracie keeps her eyes on the horizon. Caleb takes notice.

                    CALEB
              (softly)
          What are you gazing at?

Tears of desperation flow down her face.

261   **EXT. AMISH COUNTRY - DAY**

A passenger bus passes by an Amish buggy.

262   **INT. PASSENGER BUS - DAY**

Jake, Sensei Yumi, and Bark sit in the front row next to the BUS
DRIVER. Jake's left arm is bandaged in a brace.

                    SENSEI YUMI
          Hope we not too late.

                    JAKE
          I hope so too.

The bus is filled with World War II Veterans and their wives.

263   **EXT. JACOBS' FARM - DAY**

Gracie continues to eye the horizon.

                    CALEB
                (softly)
        What do you keep gazing at, woman?

Gracie cries, but doesn't say a thing.

                    FATHER BISHOP
        ...approaching marriage in accordance
        with our Biblical teachings?

                    CALEB
        Yes.

                    FATHER BISHOP
        Gracie, you have to say, yes?

Gracie continues to cry, but does not say a word.

                    FATHER BISHOP
        Gracie?

                    CALEB
        She is overjoyed with tears of
        happiness. You may continue.

Father Bishop looks over at Mr. Jacobs. Mr. Jacobs gives him a
grieving nod. Father Bishop continues.

264   **INT. PASSENGER BUS - DAY**

VETERAN MAN(in his 80's) sees JAKE. VETERAN WIFE(in her 80's} sits
beside him.

                    VETERAN MAN
                (to Jake)
        Pardon the intrusion, Sonny, but aren't
        you Jake Daniels, the person that won
        the karate championship last night?

                    JAKE
        That's me, yes.

                    VETERAN MAN
                (to everyone on bus)
        HEY! LISTEN UP, EVERYBODY! JAKE
        "THE NICE" DANIELS IS ON THIS BUS.

Everyone cheers and greets Jake and Sensei Yumi.

                    VETERAN WIFE
        Well, why didn't you say so sooner!?
                (to Bus Driver)
        BUS DRIVER STEP ON IT! WE'VE GOT A
        WEDDING TO CRASH!

265   **EXT. JACOBS' FARM - DAY**

CALEB & GRACIE'S POSITION:

>   FATHER BISHOP(O.S.)
> ...regardless of any difficult
> circumstances that may arise, until
> God will separate you by death?

>   CALEB
> Yes.

Gracie grieves her heart with tears, but does not respond. Father
Bishop looks over at Mr. Jacobs.

MR. JACOBS' POSITION:

Mrs. Jacobs takes comfort in Mr. Jacobs arms.

266   **INT. PASSENGER BUS - DAY**

>   JAKE
> That's the place right there. The
> one with all the buggies!

267   **EXT. JACOBS' FARM - DAY**

CALEB & GRACIE'S POSITION:

Tears of despair roll down Gracie's cheeks, as Father Bishop
continues the ceremony.

>   FATHER BISHOP(O.S.)
> ...and may all of your days be spent
> together to honor God, each other, and
> your family with your divine love. This
> be done through our Lord and Savior,
> Jesus Christ, Amen.

>   EVERYONE
> Amen.

>   FATHER BISHOP
> Brother Caleb, you may kiss your wife.

Caleb eagerly goes in for a kiss, when suddenly...

BUS HORN: HONK-HONKKKKKKKKKKKKKKKKKKKKKKKKK!!!!

An expression of hope forms on Gracie's face.

>   GRACIE
>   (softly to herself)
> It's Isaac.

She tries to flee, but Caleb has a firm grip on her arm.

(CONTINUED)

                              CALEB
                          (rudely)
                Where are you going, wife?

                             GRACIE
                Let go of me.

She forcefully pulls her arm and breaks free.

JAKE'S POSITION:

Bus pulls in abruptly. Door swings open, revealing Jake.
Jake(arm bandaged) and Gracie run toward each other until they
embrace each other. She pecks him 3 kisses on the cheek and
squeezes him tightly with love.

                             JAKE
                Ouch-ouch! Not so hard! Not so hard!!!

Tears of joy run down Gracie's face.

                             GRACIE
                You came for me!

                             JAKE
                How could I not? I love you, Gracie.

                             GRACIE
                And I love you.

CALEB'S POSITION:

Caleb burns fiercely with a jealousy and anger.

                             CALEB
                Isaac has just defiled my wife.
                Someone do something!

JAKE & GRACIE'S POSITION:

As they continue to hold each other with love, a sudden
sadness comes over her. The embrace ends.

                             GRACIE
                Oh no. Oh no, Isaac.

                             JAKE
                What's wrong?

                             GRACIE
                I have already been given into
                marriage to Caleb.

                             JAKE
                          (confused)
                You said "yes" to him?

A look of confusion forms on her face.

(CONTINUED)

> GRACIE
> I did not say "yes." I did not say
> anything.

> JAKE
> Then how can you be married?

Moment of silence as she ponders for a moment.

> GRACIE
> Yes... Yes, you are right! Let us ask.

FATHER BISHOP'S POSITION:

Gracie and Jake walk over to Father Bishop.

> CALEB
> (with anger)
> Give me back my wife, you rotten—

Caleb wants to grab Gracie by force, but Jake takes a step
in front of her.

> JAKE
> Take another step and you won't be
> taking another. I promise you that.

> CALEB
> (to everyone)
> Just listen to his threats! How can
> anyone stand for this lawlessness?

> JAKE
> (to Caleb)
> It's not a threat. It's protecting
> what I love from wolves like you.

Caleb backs down in fear.

> JAKE
> (to Father Bishop)
> Is it not in your laws that the
> marriage vows need to be verbal in
> the presence of all?

> FATHER BISHOP
> That is correct, yes.

> JAKE
> (to Father Bishop)
> So by your own admission, Gracie
> has become the first sister in your
> community to be married without a
> verbal approval. Is this true?

A look of shame forms on Father Bishop's face. He glances
over at the Elders. The Elders talk between themselves.

268   **INT. PASSENGER BUS - DAY**

EVERYONE on the bus is looking out the window.

                    VETERAN WIFE
                 (to Veteran Man)
              Looks like he just stirred the pot?

                    BUS DRIVER(V.O.)
              We need everyone to get back in
              their seats. I'm on a time schedule.

Everyone on the bus makes disapproving gestures and noises.

269   **EXT. JACOBS' FARM - DAY**

Caleb notices he is losing favor with the crowd.

                    CALEB
              How can we stand for this lack of respect
              for our laws and our traditions? What kind
              of people are we becoming? Shall we allow
              this wretched English man to dictate how
              we ought to live our lives? I say to you
              now, do not allow this man- this unworthy
              outsider to bully us into submission.

                    JAKE
              You are the real bully, Caleb. Somehow
              you forced Gracie's father into giving
              her to you.

                    CALEB
              Your fighting ways have made you
              completely mad, Isaac.

                    JAKE
              Just admit it, Caleb!

                    CALEB
                 (to everyone)
              Someone take courage and stand up
              to this worthless outsider!

                    JAKE
              ADMIT IT!

MR. JACOBS' POSITION:

                    MR. JACOBS
              ENOUGH!!!

It becomes quiet. Mr. Jacobs walks up to Jake and Gracie.

                    MR. JACOBS
                 (to everyone)
              I have something of deep importance to
              confess to everyone present here today.

                                        (CONTINUED)

                              GRACIE
                    No, Father.

                              MR. JACOBS
                    It must be done, my daughter. I can
                    not hide it any longer. This should
                    have been done long ago.

Mr. Jacobs turns to the people, walking around as he speaks.

                              MR. JACOBS
                    I (sigh) I was not always a brother.
                    In fact, a little over 30 years ago,
                    I used to live in Akron, Ohio selling
                    cars for a living.

Everyone's shocked by the admission.

                              MR. JACOBS
                    My real name was Brian. Brian Sabony.
                    I was an English man, just like Isaac,
                    but through God's providence, I fell in
                    love with my lovely Amish bride, Leah
                    Jacobs. Against everyone's will, we got
                    married and I took her name. We used to
                    live in Millersburg, but we were shunned
                    by everyone, including her own family. We
                    moved here and started a new life together,
                    with the hopes that we could forever
                    abandon our past. But looks like today
                    our past has finally caught up with us.

Mrs. Jacobs comes to her husband's side and holds him.

                              ELLA
                    Is this true, mother?

                              MRS. JACOBS
                    Yes, my daughter. It is true.

                              ELLA
                         (with grief)
                    Oh mother. Why did you not tell us?

Ella holds her mother for comfort.

                              MR. JACOBS
                    Caleb discovered our hidden secret
                    and used it against me, against my
                    family, to force me to give Gracie
                    into marriage.

                              CALEB
                         (to everyone)
                    I do not know what this man is
                    talking about. He is making it up.

                              MR. JACOBS
                    I did not want to give Gracie to him,
                    but as Isaac has said, I was forced
                         (MORE)

                          MR. JACOBS(cont'd)
             against my will, because I feared that if
             the truth became known, my whole family
             would have been shunned and shamed.

                          CALEB
                    (to everyone)
             He is lying! You have to believe me.

                          MR. JACOBS
             Now that you have all heard the
             truth about my family, about who we
             are, it is in your hands to decide
             what will happen between us from
             this day forth. I love my family and
             I love you as my brothers and sisters,
             and if you would accept us as we are,
             I would like us to continue to live
             among you, and to worship our Lord
             Jesus Christ together.

People talk among themselves for a tad. Gracie embraces Mr. Jacobs.

                          GRACIE
             I am so proud of you, Father.

                          MR. JACOBS
                    (to Gracie)
             The truth has set me free, my daughter.
             Only regret is not doing it sooner.

CHIEF ELDER'S POSITION:

                          CHIEF ELDER
             I call all Elders together for a
             special meeting.

The Elders gather in a circle a few yards away.

CALEB'S FATHER'S POSITION:

                          CALEB
                    (to everyone)
             This is horse dung! Pure horse
             dung, I tell you!
                    (to Caleb's Father)
             Let us go, Father. I do not want to
             hear any more of this utter rubbish.

Caleb's Father walks up to Caleb, looks directly into his eyes, and
smacks him hard across the face, just once.

                          CALEB'S FATHER
                    (with rebuke)
             You have disgraced me and you have
             disgraced my family. You are not
             worthy to be called my son.

Holding his cheek in disgrace, Caleb hesitantly backs away,
then runs off. Caleb's Father approaches Mr. Jacobs with
deep shame. He eyes the ground the whole time.

                                                      (CONTINUED)

> CALEB'S FATHER
> I apologize for my son's disgrace,
> Brother Jacobs. His sins are guilty
> against my family, and against
> yours, and against our God. I am
> deeply ashamed for what he has done.
> Will you forgive us?

Mr. Jacobs gives Caleb's Father a strong encouraging hug.

> MR. JACOBS
> What has transpired here today had
> nothing to do with you. Be in peace,
> my brother.

JAKE'S POSITION:

Samuel gives Jake a strong manly embrace.

> SAMUEL
> Good to see you again, Isaac.

> JAKE
> It's good to see you.

Abe and Ariel come over to Jake.

> JAKE
> (to Abe)
> My brother.

Jake gives Abe a strong manly embrace too.

> ABE
> I want you to meet my bride to be.

> JAKE
> (surprised)
> Ariel!?

Abe and Ariel gaze into each other's eyes with delight.

> ARIEL
> In a month's time it will be official.

> JAKE
> Congratulations to both of you.

> ABE   ARIEL
> Thank you.   Thank you.

Mr. Jacobs and Gracie enter.

> MR. JACOBS
> Welcome back, Isaac.

Jake kneels before Mr. Jacobs.

                         JAKE
          Mr. Jacobs, I beg you to hear me. In the
          little time I spent among you I have
          fallen in love with your daughter. She
          has saved me in more ways than I know. It
          broke my heart when I had to leave, but in
          the end it was for the best, because now
          I know that everything I need, and
          everything I want in life, is right here
          among you. If you permit me to marry
          your daughter, I will become one of you.
          Just as you did for Mrs. Jacobs, I will do
          for your daughter. What do you say?

                         MR. JACOBS
          You may rise, Isaac.

Jake gets up. Mr. Jacobs give Jake a strong hug.

                         JAKE
          Is that a yes?

                         CHIEF ELDER(O.S.)
          May I have your undivided attention.

CHIEF ELDER'S POSITION:

Everyone has their eyes and ears glued to Chief Elder.

                         CHIEF ELDER
          It is of our opinion that because Brother
          Jacobs has lived among us all these years,
          and has proven that he has put his English
          ways aside and has embraced our culture,
          our traditions, our God, and our way of life,
          for all these long years, our unanimous
          decision is that his family may continue to
          dwell among us, and continue to be one of us,
          as before. If we would have decided any
          differently, our community would have
          grieved deeply for years.

Everyone celebrates.

                         CHIEF ELDER
          Now, as for Caleb and Gracie, we have come
          to the decision that no marriage has taken
          place, for according to our laws, in order
          for a marriage to be made valid, a verbal
          agreement must indeed be present from both
          parties, which has not happened here.

Gracie embraces Jake with joy.

                         CHIEF ELDER
          Gracie and Isaac, come forward.

JAKE & GRACIE'S POSITION:

Jake takes Gracie's hand and approaches Chief Elder.

(CONTINUED)

> CHIEF ELDER
> It is also of our opinion that Gracie
> has defiled herself by embracing a man
> as a woman would embrace her husband.
>   (to Gracie)
> Do you deny this, Sister Gracie?

> GRACIE
> I do not deny it. It is as you say.

> FATHER BISHOP
> And what do you desire to do about
> this defilement?

> GRACIE
> If it pleases the Elders, I would
> like to marry him.

> JAKE
>   (jokingly)
> I can live with that.

Slight laughter forms across the congregation.

> CHIEF ELDER
>   (to everyone)
> SILENCE!
>   (to Jake)
> Have you accepted Jesus Christ as
> your personal Lord and Savior, Isaac?

> JAKE
> Yes, Gracie had a lot to do with my
> decision to follow our Lord Jesus.

They look into each other's eyes with love.

> CHIEF ELDER
>   (to Jake)
> You do realize that if we allow this
> marriage to take life, you will be
> bound to an oath before God and before
> this congregation to become one of
> us for the rest of your earthly life?

> JAKE
> Yes, I understand. I will abide by
> your teachings and your traditions
> for as long as I live.

> CHIEF ELDER
> Brother Jacobs, it is our recommendation
> that these two be bound together into
> marriage. What is your word?

MR. JACOBS' POSITION:

> MR. JACOBS
> They both have our blessing.

Mrs. Jacobs holds Mr. Jacobs with love and adoration.

                                              (CONTINUED)

JAKE & GRACIE'S POSITION:

> CHIEF ELDER
> So be it!

He gives the nod to Father Bishop. Father Bishop takes over.

> FATHER BISHOP
> Isaac and Gracie, do you both confess and
> believe that God has ordained marriage
> to be a covenant between one husband and...

270   **INT. PASSENGER BUS - DAY**

EVERYONE on the bus celebrates with whistles and cheers.

VETERAN MAN POSITION:

Veteran Man and Veteran Wife look out the window.

> VETERAN WIFE
> Awwwww! I love happy endings.

> VETERAN MAN
> Hey toots? Wanna go schmoozing with
> me tonight?

Veteran Man looks at his wife, jiggling his eyebrows up and down.

> VETERAN WIFE
> (infuriated)
> How dare you talk to me that way!?
> (to Bus Driver)
> BUS DRIVER! STEP ON IT!

She looks out the window furious, but after a moment a smirky smile
forms on her lips, as she peeks at him from the corner of her eyes.

271   **EXT. JACOBS' FARM - DAY**

CHARITY'S POSITION:

Tears flow down Charity's face. Sarah stands beside her.

> SARAH
> This is so romantic.

> CHARITY
> I know!

Charity takes comfort in Sarah's arms.

JAKE & GRACIE'S POSITION:

Gracie's hand sits over Jake's hand, as they gaze into each other's
eyes with delight. Tears of joy and happiness slide down her face.

> FATHER BISHOP
> ...May he richly pour his blessings
> upon you, and may all of your days be
> spent together to honor God, each other,
> and your family with your divine love.
> This be done through our Lord and
> Savior, Jesus Christ, Amen.

> EVERYONE
> Amen!

> FATHER BISHOP
> Isaac, you may kiss your bride.

> JAKE
> Don't mind if I do.

Jake and Gracie share a wonderful heartfelt kiss.

MONTAGE SHOTS:

While Jake and Gracie are sharing their kiss. A quick montage of
other people celebrating their marriage, is seen. Sensei Yumi and
Bark, Timmy, Amish Teen #1, Amish Teen #2, and other brothers and
sisters in the community.

MR. JACOBS' POSITION:

Mrs. Jacobs cries happily. Mr. Jacobs holds her for comfort.

> MR. JACOBS
> God truly watched out for us. What
> say you, Mrs. Jacobs?

Mrs. Jacobs cries even harder.

> MR. JACOBS
> There-there, now. It could have
> been worse, you know.

JAKE & GRACIE'S POSITION:

Their kiss comes to an end.

> JAKE
> (softly)
> Was it worth the wait, Mrs. Daniels?

> GRACIE
> (softly)
> Definitely, Mr. Daniels!

Gracie and Jake walk through the crowd as people congratulate them.

VOCAL FAITH SONG BEGINS...

SUPER WIDE SHOT:

We crane up from the wedding, to see the bus driving away in the
background towards the village of Mt. Joy.

(CONTINUED)

PRODUCTION CREDITS ROLL ON SCREEN:

===

AUTHOR: Victor, L. Sabadus

===
===

CHIEF EDITOR: Kurtis Zetouna

===

SECONDARY EDITORS: Nikita de Castro

                    Daniel Cioarca

                    Benjamin Dacin

                    Stefan Ghinescu

                    Jeffrey Paul Koss

                    Estee Lipenholtz

                    Elijah Lovell

                    Sierra Okoniewski

                    Bo Chateau Opatick

                    Chris Pope

                    Beniamin Sabadus

                    Maisie Talboys

                    Josh Yuchasz

                    Ashley Zetouna

                    Matthew Zuby

===

THANKS AND APPRECIATION: Elvira Sabadus

                          Dumitru Sabadus

                          Alexandra Popa

                          Dana Popa

===

VOCAL FAITH SONG ENDS.

                        "THE END"

I, Victor, would like to thank all those who has been a part
of this 3+ year project. It has been quite a challenge, but
it's finally finished! God Bless you all, and thank-you again.

Printed in the United States
By Bookmasters